A PLAIN MAN'S GUIDE
TO HOLINESS

A PLAIN MAN'S GUIDE TO HOLINESS

(ORIGINALLY PUBLISHED AS A PLAIN ACCOUNT OF CHRISTIAN PERFECTION)

John Wesley

Edited by
Halcyon C. Backhouse

HODDER AND STOUGHTON
LONDON SYDNEY AUCKLAND TORONTO

British Library Cataloguing in Publication Data

Wesley, John, *1703–1791*
  [A plain account of Christian perfection.] A plain man's guide to
holiness.
  1. Christian doctrine. Holiness
  I. [A plain account of Christian perfection]. II. Title III. Backhouse,
Halcyon C.
  234

  ISBN 0 340 41501 0

*Hodder & Stoughton Editorial Office: 47 Bedford Square, London
WC1B 3DP.*

Contents

Introduction

John Wesley

John Wesley was born on June 17th, 1703 in the remote village of Epworth, in the Lincolnshire fens. He was the most celebrated member of the talented Wesley family, the son of a clergyman, Samuel Wesley, and an outstanding mother, Susanna, who personally undertook the primary education of her ten children. Few would have thought that ten thousand people would file past the coffin after her son's death eighty-seven years later, on March 2nd, 1791 at his home in City Road, London.

At the age of 17, after the rigours of Charterhouse School – which Wesley later felt had been good preparation for his subsequent tough itinerant life – Wesley arrived at Christ Church, Oxford, on a £40.00-a-year scholarship. In 1726, after his ordination in the Church of England, Wesley became a curate to his father. That same year his younger brother Charles, later to be nicknamed 'the sweet singer' of Methodism because of the many hymns he wrote ('Love divine, all loves excelling', 'Hark, the herald angels sing', and 'Christ the Lord is risen today' being among his most well-known hymns), arrived in Oxford and later formed a group which became known as the 'Holy Club'. When John Wesley returned to Oxford he took over the leadership of this group of 'serious' students (which included the son of a Gloucester innkeeper, George Whitefield, whom Charles Wesley advised on which Christian books he should read). The Holy Club met for Bible study, prayer, self-examination: its members paid for food and clothing for the destitute in Oxford, went to the prisons, and visited people in appalling conditions in the workhouses. Their overriding aim was to put into practice the command, 'Love your neighbour as yourself'.

John and Charles Wesley established a pattern of serving and working together. They sought together, from the start, God's guidance and strength, as they founded, organised, pastored, taught, and provided the hymn-books for what was later known as 'Methodism'. Students of modern church growth movements today find this quite remarkable by any standards.

The brothers spent two years as missionaries in Georgia but returned with a sense of failure. On board John Wesley's boat back to England there were a group of German peasants, known as Moravians, whose simple Christian faith greatly impressed this English clergyman. In that same year John Wesley was also greatly helped by talking with another Moravian, Peter Böhler. Three days after this conversation, on May 24th, 1738, Wesley reluctantly attended a meeting in Aldersgate Street where he experienced what has subsequently become one of the most oft-quoted instances of a 'conversion' experience. John Wesley himself describes how he heard Luther's *Preface to the Romans* being read aloud and felt his heart being 'strangely warmed'. He always thought of this moment as his 'spiritual birthday' and wrote, 'I felt I did trust in Christ, Christ alone, for salvation; and an assurance was given me that he had taken away *my* sins, even mine, and saved me from the law of sin and death.'

That spiritual experience transformed John Wesley's life. All his subsequent preaching altered. He was soon unwelcome in many churches, and, encouraged by George Whitefield, he preached in the open air to huge crowds of ordinary people. In this Wesley did something unheard of for an Anglican minister. He became a 'field preacher'. It has been estimated that he travelled some quarter of a million miles on horseback, preaching over

40,000 sermons, often two, three or four a day, for almost the next fifty years. Consequent upon his conversion, Wesley responded to the divine call to preach the gospel to every creature. His aim was clearly etched in his mind. He had pinpointed his objective. John Wesley set out to 'reform the nation, particularly the Church, and to spread Scriptural holiness over the land' (Wesley, *Works*, Vol. VIII, p. 299).[1]

The birth of Methodism

Many thousands of people responded and became Christians. There was no place for them, and they were not wanted by the established Anglican churches, but they needed spiritual guidance and care. So 'Methodists' were organised into 'classes' of ten people who were under a 'class leader'. John Wesley wrote that the job of a class leader was: 'to see each person in his class once a week, at least, in order to inquire how their souls prosper; to advise, reprove, comfort or exhort, as occasion may require: to receive what they may be willing to give to the poor.'[2]

Wesley split the country into areas, and appointed preachers to these 'circuits'. He kept a firm hand on the organisation of Methodism through the Methodist Conferences, to which he invited the preachers.

As a result, John Wesley became perhaps the most well-known figure, among all classes of society, in the eighteenth century. More importantly it resulted in a phenomenal revival of Christianity, especially among the working classes. John Wesley spoke of the exceptional 'extent of the movement' in his famous sermon marking the foundation of the City Road Chapel, London:

This revival of religion spread to such a degree as neither we nor our fathers had known. How *extensive* has it been! There is scarce a considerable town in the kingdom where some have not been made witnesses of it. It has spread to every age and sex, to most orders and degrees of men; and even to abundance of those who, in time past, were accounted monsters of wickedness.[3]

Christian Perfection

'Christian Perfection' is not a phrase we use very much today. 'Holiness' and 'sanctification' are John Wesley's synonyms for 'Christian Perfection', and these might be more familiar, hence the title given to this new edition of John Wesley's book, which first appeared under the title: *A plain account of Christian Perfection*.

Wesley states that his aim in this book is to give an account of the steps by which he was led to embrace the doctrine of Christian Perfection. As he does this he gives the reader interesting insights into early Methodism, including summaries of the first four Methodist Conferences, and his first published sermon. He also cites a number of his own and Charles Wesley's hymns from their early hymn-books.

Wesley's deep concern in the interior life and the spiritual pilgrimage of the Christian was set alight when he read Bishop Taylor's *Rules and Exercises of Holy Living and Dying*, Thomas à Kempis's *Christian's Pattern*, and William Law's two books, *Christian Perfection* and *Serious Call*. The two other major influences which fanned the flames for the doctrine of Christian Perfection were his own study of the Bible, and his meeting with the German Arvid Gradin, during which he discovered Gradin's seemingly revolutionary definition of 'the full assurance of faith'.

A basic Christian doctrine

Wesley consistently taught that a 'perfect Christian would be one who rejoiced, prayed and gave thanks in all circumstances'. This he highlights from the personal experience of a fellow Christian. In Chapter 24, Jane Cooper's letter is held up as a clear example of a Christian who has genuinely embraced the doctrine of perfection. It is also a most moving account of how one Christian faced up to and coped with dying from the very painful disease of smallpox, unaided by drugs and modern medicines.

Bible usage

Topics such as renewal, sinless perfection, speaking in tongues, predicting the precise date of the end of the world, all have a modern ring, and are among some of the issues which Wesley deals with in his book. He directly quotes many hundreds of scriptural references and makes allusions to many more.

In all of Wesley's teaching his arguments are clinched by one or more pertinent Bible references. For this edition of Wesley's book Bible references have been taken from the *New International Version*. However, the reader will become aware that at some of the most critical points in Wesley's argument the *Authorised Version* (AV) of the Bible exactly supports Wesley, but that the *New International Version* (NIV) of the Bible introduces the possibility of a different, and sometimes crucially different, interpretation. On these relatively few occasions both the AV and the NIV translations have been given.

This unabridged edition of Wesley's writings on Christian Perfection is based on the third edition of *Wesley's*

Works, Volume XI, which was originally published by John Mason of 14 City Road, London, in 1830. In this edition Wesley's hymns have been left unaltered, and his sermons and extracts from his own previously published works have only been altered where archaic words or phrases obscure the meaning of Wesley's writings. Elsewhere there has been slight editing – again with the simple intention of making Wesley's meaning clear to the present-day reader.

A challenge for today

For any Christian, of whatever denominational background, Wesley remains a force to be contended with. Most of his teaching in this book is uncontroversial. His clear, rigorous exposition focuses on the Christian's individual walk with God. For Wesley it begins and ends in love. Throughout we read an astonishing account of a visionary's heart. This may be summed up in his own words: 'The more care should we take to keep the simple scriptural account in view. Pure love reigning alone in the heart and life, this is the whole of Christian Perfection.'

The clearest guide to spiritual perfection is found in Jesus's own words: 'The most important one [commandment] . . . is this: "Hear, O Israel, the Lord our God, the Lord is one. Love the Lord your God with all your heart and with all your soul and with all your mind and with all your strength." The second is this: "Love your neighbour as yourself." There is no commandment greater than these' (Mark 12:29–31).

Unpack those words into daily living and we have a Wesleyan tract of 1777! That mystical concept of love between man and God through Christ Jesus stamps this work. And the message of the Rev. John Wesley still thunders today encouraging his hearers to make the same complete commitment in Christian living.

Notes

[1] *The Inextinguishable Blaze*, A. Skevington Wood, Paternoster Press, 1960, p. 163.
[2] *Chalmers's Biographical Dictionary*, Vol. XXXI, 1817 p. 306.
[3] Quoted in *The Inextinguishable Blaze*, p. 235.

Halcyon Backhouse

It is not to be understood, that Mr Wesley's sentiments concerning Christian Perfection were in any measure changed after the year 1777. This tract underwent several revisions and enlargements during his life-time; and in every successive edition the date of the most recent revision was specified. The last revision appears to have been made in the year 1777; and since that period, this date has been generally continued on the title-page of the several editions of the pamphlet. (Editor of *The Works of the Rev. John Wesley, A.M.* Vol. 11, Third Edition, published by John Mason, 14 City Road, London, 1830.)

A PLAIN ACCOUNT OF CHRISTIAN PERFECTION, AS BELIEVED AND TAUGHT BY THE REVEREND MR JOHN WESLEY, FROM THE YEAR 1724, TO THE YEAR 1777

1 Introduction

What I intend in the following papers is to give a plain and distinct account of the steps by which I was led, over a period of many years, to embrace the doctrine of Christian Perfection. I owe this to the serious section of mankind, and to those who desire to know all 'the truth as it is in Jesus'. These are only concerned with questions of this kind and to these I would plainly tell the thing as it is. I will try throughout, from one period to another, to show both what I thought, and why I thought as I did.

2 Bishop Taylor's *Rules and Exercises of Holy Living and Dying*

In 1725, when I was 23 years old, I came across Bishop Taylor's *Rules and Exercises of Holy Living and Dying*. As I read several parts of this book, I was greatly moved, especially by the part which relates to the purity of intention. Instantly, I resolved to dedicate all my life to God. All my thoughts, and words, and actions were to be God's. I was thoroughly convinced there was no middle way, but that every part of my life (not just some) must either be a sacrifice to God, or myself, which in effect, is a sacrifice to the devil.

15

Can any serious person doubt this? Or can anyone find a middle way between serving God and serving the devil?

3   Kempis's *Christian's Pattern*

In 1726, I read Kempis's *Christian's Pattern*. The nature and range of inward religion, the religion of the heart, now appeared to me in a stronger light than it had ever done before. I saw that even if I were to give all my life to God (assuming that it is possible to do this, and go no farther) it would be of no profit to me, unless I gave my heart, yes, my whole heart, to him.

I saw that 'simplicity of intention, and purity of affection', as the single goal in all we speak or do, and as one desire ruling all our mental framework, are indeed 'the wings of the soul'. Without this we can never ascend the mount of God.

4   Mr Law's *Christian Perfection* and *Serious Call*

A year or two later, Mr Law's *Christian Perfection* and *Serious Call* were given to me and these convinced me, more than ever, of the absolute impossibility of being half a Christian. I determined, through God's grace (the absolute need of which I was deeply aware) to be wholly devoted to God, to give him all my soul, my body, and my substance.

Will any thinking man say that this is carrying matters too far? Or can anyone say that anything less is due to God, who has given himself for us, than to give ourselves totally to him: all we have, and all we are?

5   Studying the Bible

In the year 1729, I began not only to read, but to study, the Bible, as the one and only standard of truth, and the only model of pure religion. So I saw, in a clearer and clearer light, the indispensable need of having 'the mind of Christ' (1 Cor. 2:16) and of walking as Christ also walked; to the extent of having, not just part but the complete mind which was in Christ. I understood clearly that walking as Christ walked, involved following Christ not only in many or in most respects, but in every way. And this is how I viewed religion at this time: as a uniform following of Christ, as a complete in- and outward conformity to our Master. More than anything else, I was afraid of twisting this law to suit myself and other people. I would not allow myself the slightest deviation from following our grand Exemplar.

6   Sermon preached on *The Circumcision of the Heart*

On January 1st, 1733, I preached in front of the University, in St Mary's church, on 'The Circumcision of the Heart'; here is an account of what I said:

It is that habitual disposition of soul which, in the sacred writings, is termed holiness; and which directly implies being cleansed from sin, 'from everything that contaminates body and spirit' (2 Cor. 7:1); and, by consequence, being endued with those virtues which were in Christ Jesus; 'to be made new in the attitude of your minds' (Eph. 4:23) and to be 'perfect ... as your heavenly Father is perfect' (Matt. 5:48).

In the same sermon I observed,

'Therefore love is the fulfilment of the law' (Rom. 13:10). 'The goal of this command is love' (1 Tim. 1:5). It is not only 'the first and greatest commandment' (Matt. 22:38), but all the commandments in one. ' . . . whatever is right, whatever is pure . . . if anything is excellent or praiseworthy' (Phil. 4:8), they are all comprised in this one word, love. In this is perfection, and glory, and happiness. The royal law of heaven and earth is this, 'Love the Lord your God with all your heart and with all your soul and with all your mind' (Matt. 22:37). The one perfect good is to be your one ultimate end. One thing will you desire for its own sake – the fruition of him who is all in all. One happiness shall you propose to your souls, even a union with him that made them, having 'fellowship . . . with the Father and with his Son' (1 John 1:3) and being united 'with the Lord . . . in spirit' (1 Cor. 6:17). You are to pursue one design to the end of time – the enjoyment of God in time and in eternity. Desire other things only so far as they tend to this; love the creature, as it leads to the Creator. But in every step you take, let this be the glorious point that terminates your view. Let every affection, every thought, every word, every action, be subordinate to this. Whatever you desire or fear, seek or shun, whatever you think, speak, or do, let it be in order for your happiness in God, the sole end, as well as source, of your being.

I concluded with these words:

Here is the sum of the perfect law, the circumcision of the heart. Let the spirit return to God that gave it, with the whole train of its affections.

Other sacrifices from us he would not accept, but the living sacrifice of the heart he has chosen. Let it be continually offered up to God through Christ, in flames of holy love. And let no creature be suffered to share with him, for he is a jealous God. He will not share his

18

throne with another; he will reign without a rival. Let no design, no desire be admitted there, other than God for its ultimate object. This is the way those children of God once walked, who though dead still speak to us: 'Desire not to live but to praise his name; let all your thoughts, words, and works tend to his glory.' 'Let your soul be filled with so entire a love for him, that you may love nothing but for his sake.' 'Have a pure intention of heart, a steadfast regard to his glory in all your actions.' 'For then, and not till then, is that mind in us, which was in Christ Jesus, when in every prompting of our heart, in every word of our tongue, in every work of our hands, we pursue nothing that is not in relation to him, and in subordination to his pleasure;' when we also neither think, speak, nor act, to fulfil 'our own will, but the will of him who sent us' (see John 6:38); when, 'whether we eat or drink, or whatever we do,' we do it all 'to the glory of God' (See 1 Cor. 10:31).

It may be noted that this sermon was the first of all my writings which were published. This was the view of religion I then had. Even then I did not hesitate to use the word *perfection*. This is the view I have of it now, without any material addition or subtraction. And what is there here which any man of understanding, who believes the Bible, can object to? What can he deny, without flatly contradicting the Scripture? What can he cut out, without taking away from the word of God?

7   'O may thy love possess me whole'

In the same sentiment my brother and I remained (with all those young men who were derided and nicknamed *Methodists*) until we set sail for America, in the latter part of 1735. It was the next year, while I was at Savannah, that I wrote the following lines:

Is there a thing beneath the sun,
That strives with thee my heart to share?
Ah! tear it thence, and reign alone,
The Lord of every motion there!

In the beginning of the year 1738, as I was returning from there, the cry of my heart was,

O grant that nothing in my soul
May dwell, but thy pure love alone!
O may thy love possess me whole,
My joy, my treasure, and my crown;
Strange fires far from my heart remove;
My every act, word, thought, be love!

I never heard that anyone objected to this. And indeed who can object? Is not this the language, not only of every believer, but of every one who is truly awakened? To this day, have I written anything that is stronger or plainer than this?

8 Arvid Gradin's definition of 'full assurance of faith'

In the following August I had a long conversation with Arvid Gradin in Germany. After he had given me an account of his experience, I desired him to give me, in writing, a definition of 'full assurance of faith' (Heb. 10:22). He did in the following words:

Requies in sanguine Christi; firma fiducia in Deum, et persuasio de gratia divina; tranquillitas mentis summa, atque serenitas et pax; cum absentia omnis desiderii carnalis, et cessatione peccatorum etiam internorum.

(Repose in the blood of Christ; a firm confidence in God, and persuasion of his favour; the highest tranquillity, serenity, and peace of mind, with a deliverance from every fleshly desire, and a cessation of all, even inward sins.)

This was the first account I ever heard from any living person of what I had previously learned for myself from the actual words of God. And this I had been praying for (with my small company of friends) and expecting, for several years.

9 John and Charles Wesley's *Hymns and Sacred Poems*

In 1739, my brother and I published a volume of *Hymns and Sacred Poems*. In many of these we declared our feelings strongly and explicitly. So:

> Turn the full stream of nature's tide!
> Let all our actions tend
> To thee, their source: thy love the guide,
> Thy glory be the end.
> Earth then a scale to heaven shall be;
> Sense shall point out the road;
> The creatures all shall lead to thee,
> And all we taste be God.

Again:

> Lord, arm me with thy Spirit's might,
> Since I am call'd by thy great name:
> In thee my wand'ring thoughts unite,
> Of all my works be thou the aim:
> Thy love attend me all my days,
> And my sole business be thy praise.

Again:

Eager for thee I ask and pant;
So strong the principle divine,
Carries me out with sweet constraint,
Till all my hallow'd soul be thine;
Plunged in the Godhead's deepest sea,
And lost in thine immensity!

And one more:

Heavenly Adam, life divine,
Change my nature into thine;
Move and spread throughout my soul,
Actuate and fill the whole.

It would be easy to cite many more similar passages, but these are sufficient to show, beyond contradiction, what our views then were.

10   The Character of a Methodist

The first tract I ever wrote specifically on this subject was published at the latter end of 1739. So that no one might be prejudiced before they read it, I gave it the impartial title of *The Character of a Methodist*. In this I described a perfect Christian, and at the front of the book, I put this quotation: 'Not that I have already obtained all this' (Phil 3:12). Part of it now follows without any alteration:

A Methodist is one who loves the Lord his God with all his heart, with all his soul, with all his mind, and with all his strength. God is the joy of his heart, and the desire of his soul, which is continually crying, 'Whom have I in heaven but you? And earth has nothing I desire besides you' (Ps. 73:25). My God and my all! 'God is the strength of my heart and my portion for ever' (Ps. 73:26). He is therefore happy in God; yes, always happy, as having in him a well of water springing up to everlasting life, and overflowing his soul with peace and joy. Now that perfect love has driven out fear (see 1 John 4:18), he rejoices evermore. Yes, his joy is full, and all his bones cry out, 'Praise be to the God and Father of our Lord Jesus Christ, who, in his great mercy has given me new birth in a living hope of an inheritance that can never perish, spoil or fade – kept in heaven for me' (see 1 Pet. 1:3–4).

And he, who has this hope, thus full of immortality, giving thanks in all circumstances, knowing that this is God's will (whatever it is) for him in Christ Jesus (see 1 Thess. 5:18). From him therefore he cheerfully receives all, saying, 'The will of the Lord is good;' and he blesses the name of the Lord in the same way, whether the Lord gives or takes away. Whether in ease or pain, whether in sickness or health, whether in life or death, he gives thanks from the bottom of his heart to him who orders it for good; into whose hands he has completely committed his body and soul, as into the hands of a 'faithful Creator' (see 1 Pet. 4:19). He is therefore not anxious about anything (see Phil. 4:6) as he has 'cast all his anxiety on him because he cares for him' (see 1 Pet. 5:7), and 'in everything' relying on him, after he has presented his requests to God 'with thanksgiving' (see Phil. 4:6).

For indeed he 'pray[s] continually' (1 Thess. 5:17); at all times the language of his heart is this, 'To you is my mouth, though without a voice; and my silence speaks to you.' His heart is lifted up to God at all times, and in all places. In this he is never hindered, much less inter-rupted, by any person or thing. Alone or in company, in leisure, business, or in conversation, his heart is ever with the Lord. When he goes to bed or gets up, God is in all his thoughts. He walks with God continually, hav-ing the loving eye of his soul fixed on him, and everywhere he sees him 'who is invisible' (Heb. 11:27).

And loving God, he 'loves his neighbour as himself' (see Mark 12:33), he loves every man as his own soul.

He loves his enemies, yes, and the enemies of God. And if it be not in his power to 'do good to them who hate' him, yet he does not cease to 'pray for them' though they reject his love, and still 'ill-treat him, and persecute him' (see Matt. 5:44; Luke 6:28).

For he is 'pure in heart' (Matt. 5:8). Love has purified his heart from envy, malice, anger, and every unkind temper. It has cleansed him from pride which 'only breeds quarrels' (Prov. 13:10), and he has now 'compassion, kindness, humility, gentleness and patience' (Col. 3:12). And indeed all possible ground for contention, on his part, is cut off. For none can take from him what he desires, 'Do not love the world or anything in the world' (1 John 2:15), but his desire is directed towards God and to the remembrance of his name.

Agreeable to this his one desire, is the one design of his life, namely, 'to do, not his own will, but the will of him who sent him' (see John 6:38). His one intention at all times and in all places is not to please himself, but him whom his soul loves. He has a good eye, and because his 'eye is good, his whole body also is full of light. The whole body is full of light as when the light of a lamp shines on it' (see Luke 11:34–6). God reigns alone, all that is in the soul is 'holy to the Lord' (see Jer. 2:3). There is not a movement in his heart which is not according to God's will. Every thought that comes points to God, and is 'in obedience to the law of Christ'.

And the tree is known by its fruits. For, as he loves God, so he 'obeys his commands' (see John 15:10), not just some of the commands, but all of them, from the least to the greatest. He is not content to 'keep the whole law and stumble at just one point' (see Jas. 2:10), but has in all points his 'conscience clear before God and man' (Acts 24:16). Whatever God has forbidden, he avoids; whatever God has enjoined, he does. 'He walks in obedience to his commands' (see 2 John 6) now God has set his heart free. It is his glory and joy so to do; it is his daily crown of rejoicing, to 'do God's will on earth as it is done in heaven' (see Matt. 6:10).

So he keeps all of God's commandments with all his strength, for his obedience is in proportion to his love, the source from whence it flows. And therefore, loving God with all his heart, he serves him with all his strength. He continually presents his soul and 'body a living sacrifice, holy and pleasing to God' (see Rom. 12:1), entirely and without reserve devoting himself, all he has, all he is, to God's glory. All the talents he has, he constantly employs according to his Master's will; every power and faculty of his soul, every member of his body.

As a result, 'whatever he did, it is all for the glory of God' (see 1 Cor. 10:31). In all his employments of every kind, he not only aims at this, which is implied in having a good eye, but actually attains it; his business and his refreshments, as well as his prayers, all serve to this great end. Whether he stays indoors or goes outside, whether he lies down, or gets up, he is promoting, in all he speaks or does, the one business of his life. Whether he put on his apparel, or labour, or eat and drink, or divert himself from too wasting labour, it all tends to advance the glory of God, by peace and goodwill among men. His one invariable rule is this: 'And whatever you do, whether in word or deed, do it all in the name of the Lord Jesus, giving thanks to God the Father through him' (Col. 3:17).

Nor do the customs of the world at all hinder him 'running the race marked out before him' (see Heb. 12:1). He cannot therefore 'store up things for himself' (Luke 12:21), no more than he can take fire into his bosom. He cannot speak evil of his neighbour, any more than he can lie either for God or man. He cannot utter an unkind word of any one; for love keeps the door of his lips. He cannot 'speak careless words,' or 'let any unwholesome talk come out of his mouth, but only what is helpful for building others up . . . that it may benefit those who listen' (see Matt. 12:36; Eph. 4:29). But 'whatever is pure, whatever is lovely, whatever is' correctly called 'admirable' (Phil. 4:8) he thinks, speaks, and acts, 'in every way making the teaching about God our Saviour attractive' (see Titus 2:10).

These are the very words in which I set out at length, for the first time, my convictions about Christian Perfection. And is it not easy to see:

1 That this is the very point at which I aimed all along from the year 1725, and very definitely from 1730, when I began to be *homo unius libri* (a man *of one* book), regarding no other book as equal to the Bible.

2 That this is precisely the same doctrine which I believe and teach to this day; not adding one point, either to that inward or outward holiness which I maintained thirty-eight years ago. And it is the same doctrine which, by the grace of God, I have continued to teach from that time until now, as will appear to every impartial person from the extracts given below.

11   Unexpected opposition

I do not know that any writer has made any objection against this tract to this day, and for some time I did not experience much opposition on the subject, at least, not from thoughtful people. But after a time there was an outcry, and what surprised me a little, from religious men, who maintained, not that I had given a wrong account of Perfection, but that 'there is no Perfection on earth'. And further, they attacked my brother and me strongly for affirming the contrary. We hardly expected such a rough attack from these men, especially as we were clear about justification by faith, and were careful to attribute the whole of salvation solely to the grace of God. But what most surprised us was, that we were said to 'dishonour Christ', by asserting that he 'is able to save completely' (Heb. 7:25), by maintaining he will reign in our hearts alone, and subdue all things to himself.

12 Wesley, encouraged by the Bishop of London, preaches and publishes about Christian Perfection

I think it was in the second half of 1740 that I had a conversation with Dr Gibson, then Bishop of London, at Whitehall. He asked me what I meant by Perfection. I told him without any disguise or reserve. When I stopped speaking, he said, 'Mr Wesley, if that is all you mean, publish it to all the world. If any one then can refute what you say, he is free to do so.'

I answered, 'My lord, I will.' And accordingly I wrote and published the following sermon on Christian Perfection.

In this I tried hard to show:
1 In what sense Christians are not perfect.
2 In what sense Christians are perfect.

1 In what sense Christians are not perfect.

They are not perfect in knowledge. They are not free from ignorance, no, nor from mistake. We are no more to expect any living man to be infallible, than to be omniscient. They are not free from infirmities, such as weakness or slowness of understanding, irregular quickness or heaviness of imagination. Similarly, not from impropriety of language, ungracefulness of pronunciation; to which one might add a thousand nameless defects, either in conversation or behaviour. From such infirmities as these none is perfectly freed till their spirits return to God. Neither can we expect till then to be wholly freed from temptation; for 'a servant is not above his master' (see Matt. 10:24). But neither in this sense is there any absolute perfection on earth. There is no perfection in levels of attainment, because there is continual progress.

2 In what sense then are Christians perfect?

Observe, we are not now speaking of newborn baby Christians, but adult Christians. But even newborn baby Christians are so far perfect as not to commit sin. This St John affirms explicitly; and it cannot be disproved by the examples of the Old Testament. For what if the holiest of the ancient Jews did sometimes commit sin? We cannot infer from this, that 'all Christians do and must commit sin as long as they live.'

But does not the scripture say, 'A righteous man sins seven times a day?' It does not. Indeed it says, 'a righteous man falls seven times' (Prov. 24:16). But this is quite another thing. For, first, the words, *a day*, are not in the text. Secondly, here is no mention of *falling into sin* at all. What is here mentioned, is, *falling into temporal affliction*.

But elsewhere Solomon says, 'there is no-one who does not sin' (1 Kgs. 8:46). Doubtless thus it was in the days of Solomon, yes, and from Solomon to Christ there was then no man that did not sin. But whatever was the case of those under the law, we may safely affirm, with St John, that, since the gospel was given, 'anyone born of God does not continue to sin' ['whosoever is born of God sinneth not' AV] (1 John 5:18).

The privileges of Christians are in no way to be measured by what the Old Testament records concerning those who were under the Jewish dispensation; seeing that the fullness of time is now come and the Holy Spirit is now given, the great salvation of God is now brought to men by the revelation of Jesus Christ. The kingdom of heaven is now set up on earth, concerning which the Spirit of God declared of old time (so far is David from being the pattern or standard of Christian perfection), 'On that day . . . the feeblest among them will be like David, and the house of David will be like God, like the Angel of the Lord going before them' (Zech. 12:8).

But the apostles themselves committed sin. Peter by

28

pretending he did not know Christ, Paul by his sharp contention with Barnabas. Suppose they did, will you argue like this, 'If two of the apostles once committed sin, then all other Christians, in all ages, do and must commit sin as long as they live'? No, God forbid we should speak like that. They did not have to sin, the grace of God was surely sufficient for them. And it is sufficient for us at this day.

But St James says, 'We all stumble in many ways' (Jas. 3:2). True, but who are the people spoken about here? Why, the many teachers whom God had not sent, not the apostle himself, nor any real Christian. When he was using the word *we*, James was using a figure of speech, common in all other as well as the inspired writings. That the apostle could not possibly include himself, or any other true believer, appears, first, from the ninth verse, 'With the tongue we praise our Lord and Father, and with it we curse men'. Surely not we apostles! Not we believers!

Second, from the words preceding verse 2: 'Not many of you should presume to be teachers, my brothers, because you know that we who teach will be judged more strictly. We all stumble in many ways' (Jas. 3:1–2). *We!* Who? Not the apostles nor true believers, but they who were to 'be judged more strictly' because of their many offences.

And third, the verse itself proves that 'We all stumble' cannot be spoken either of all men or all Christians. For in this verse, James immediately goes on to mention a man who 'is never at fault'. This man is called 'a perfect man' and is, thus distinguished from the 'we' who stumble (Jas. 3:2).

But St John himself says, 'If we claim to be without sin, we deceive ourselves' (1 John 1:8), and, 'If we claim we have not sinned, we make him out to be a liar and his word has no place in our lives' (1 John 1:10).

I answer:

1 The tenth verse fixes the sense of the eighth

29

verse. The words, 'If we claim to be without sin' in the former, being explained by, 'If we claim we have not sinned' in the latter verse.

2   The point under consideration is not whether we have or have not sinned heretofore and neither of these verses asserts that we do sin, or commit sin now.

3   The ninth verse explains both the eighth and tenth. 'If we confess our sins, he is faithful and just and will forgive us our sins and purify us from all unrighteousness.' It is as if he had said, 'I have already affirmed, the blood of Christ purifies us from all sin.' And no man can say, 'I do not need it, I have no sin to be cleansed from.' 'If we claim to be without sin' that 'we have not sinned, we deceive ourselves' and make God a liar. But 'if we confess our sins, he is faithful and just', not only to 'forgive us our sins', but also to 'purify us from all unrighteousness', that we may 'go . . . and leave your life of sin' ['go and sin no more' AV] (John 8:11). In conformity, therefore, both to the doctrine of St John, and the whole tenor of the New Testament, we come to this conclusion: a Christian is so far perfect as not to commit sin.

This is the glorious privilege of every Christian, yes, though he be but a newborn baby Christian. But only of grown Christians can it be affirmed that they are in this sense perfect; as, second, they are freed from evil thoughts and evil frames of mind. First, 'from evil or sinful thoughts.' Indeed, where do such thoughts come from? '. . . out of men's hearts', if at all, 'come evil thoughts' (Mark 7:21). If, therefore, the heart is no longer evil, then evil thoughts no longer come out of it. For 'A good tree cannot bear bad fruit' (Matt. 7:18).

And as they are freed from evil thoughts, so likewise they are freed from an evil frame of mind. Every one of these can say, with St Paul, 'I have been crucified with Christ and I no longer live, but Christ lives in me' (Gal. 2:20), words that manifestly describe a deliverance from inward as well as from outward sin. This is expressed both negatively, 'I no longer live', my evil nature, the body of sin, is destroyed; and positively, 'Christ lives in me', and therefore all that is holy, and just, and good. Indeed, both these, 'Christ lives in me', and, 'I no longer live', are inseparably connected. For 'what fellowship can light have with darkness', or Christ with Belial (see 2 Cor. 6:14–15)?

He, therefore, who lives in these Christians has 'purified their hearts by faith' (Acts 15:9), because everyone that has Christ in him, 'the hope of glory' (Col. 1:27) . . . 'purifies himself, just as he is pure' (1 John 3:3). He is purified from pride, for Christ was humble in heart (Matt. 11:29). He is pure from selfish desire and self-will, for Christ desired only to do the will of his Father. And he is pure from anger, in the common sense of the word, for Christ was gentle and humble. I say, *in the common sense of the word*, for he is angry at sin, while he is grieved for the sinner. He is displeased with every offence against God, but has only tender compassion to the offender.

So Jesus saves his people from their sins, not only from outward sins, but from the sins of their hearts. 'True,' some say, 'but not until we die, not in this world.' No, St John says, in this way, 'Love is made complete among us so that we will have confidence on the day of judgment, because in this world we are like him.' ['Here-in is our love made perfect, that we may have boldness in the day of judgment: because as he is, so are we in this world' av.] (1 John 4:17). The apostle here, beyond all contradiction, speaks about himself and other living Christians, of whom he flatly affirms that, not only at or after death but 'in this world', they are 'like him'.

Exactly consistent with this are his words in the first chapter: 'God is light; in him there is no darkness at all . . . But if we walk in the light, as he is in the light, we have fellowship with one another, and the blood of Jesus, his Son, purifies us from all sin' (1 John 1:5, 7). And again, 'If we confess our sins, he is faithful and just and will forgive us our sins and purify us from all

31

unrighteousness' (1 John 1:9). Now, it is evident, the apostle here speaks of a deliverance wrought in this world. For he does not say, 'The blood of Christ *will* purify' (at the hour of death, or in the day of judgment), but it 'purifies', at the time present, us living Christians 'from all sin'. And it is equally evident, that if any sin remain, we are not cleansed from all sin. If *any* unrighteousness remain in the soul, it is not cleansed from all unrighteousness. Neither let any say that this relates to justification only, or the cleansing of us from the guilt of sin.

First, because this is to confuse what the apostle clearly distinguishes, who mentions first, 'to forgive us our sins', and then, 'to purify us from all unrighteousness'.

Second, because this is asserting justification by works, in the strongest sense possible. It is making all inward, as well as all outward, holiness, necessarily previous to justification. For if the cleansing here spoken of is no other than the cleansing of us from the guilt of sin, then we are not cleansed from guilt: that is, not justified, because this would then be conditioned on our walking 'in the light, as he is in the light' (1 John 1:7).

It remains, then, that Christians are saved in this world from all sin, from all unrighteousness; that they are now in such a sense perfect as not to commit sin, and to be freed from evil thoughts and evil tempers.

It was inevitable that in this kind of writing, which directly contradicted many people's favourite opinion, people who were highly regarded by others, and possibly thought highly of themselves, that some of the best of Christians (although, if these things were true, they were not Christians at all) should give great offence. Many replies or criticisms, therefore, were expected, but I was agreeably disappointed. I am not aware that any appeared and so I went quietly on my way.

13 Second volume of Hymns, published in 1741

Not long after, I think in the spring, 1741, we published a second volume of hymns. As this doctrine was still much misunderstood, and consequently misrepresented, I judged it necessary to explain this point still further. I did this in the preface which now follows:

> This great gift of God, the salvation of our souls, is no other than the image of God fresh stamped on our hearts. It is believers being 'renewed in knowledge in the image of their Creator' (Col. 3:10). God has now laid 'the axe at the root of the trees . . . purifying their hearts by faith' (see Luke 3:9; Acts 15:9), and 'cleansing all the thoughts of their hearts by the inspiration of his Holy Spirit' (Book of Common Prayer: from the Collect in The Lord's Supper or Holy Communion). Having this hope, that they will see God as he is, they 'purify themselves, as he is pure' (see 1 John 3:3), and are 'holy in all [they] do, just as he who called [them] is holy' (see 1 Pet. 1:15). Not that they have already attained all that they will attain, or are already in this sense perfect. But they daily 'go from strength to strength' (Ps. 84:7), and 'with unveiled faces all reflect the Lord's glory' as they are 'being transformed into his likeness with ever-increasing glory, which comes from the Lord, who is the Spirit' (2 Cor. 3:18).
>
> And 'where the Spirit of the Lord is, there is freedom' (2 Cor. 3:17), and Christians are 'set . . . free from the law of sin and death' (Rom. 8:2), as the children of this world do not believe, though a man declare it unto them. 'The Son has made them free' (see John 8:36), who are thus 'born of God' (John 1:13), from that great root of sin and bitterness, pride. They feel that all their 'competence comes from God' (2 Cor. 3:5), that it is he alone who is in all their thoughts

and 'works in them to will and to act according to his good purpose' (see Phil. 2:13). They feel that it is not they that speak, but the Spirit of their Father speaking in them, and that whatever they do with their hands the Father who is in them is doing the work (see John 14:10). So that God to them is all in all, and they are nothing in his sight. They are freed from self-will, as desiring nothing but the holy and perfect will of God: not supplies in want, not ease in pain [John Wesley added the following footnote to this phrase taken from his Preface: 'This is too strong. Our Lord himself desired ease in pain. He asked for it, only with resignation. "Yet not as I will, but as you will" (Matt. 26:39).'] nor life or death, or any creature; but continually crying in their inmost soul, 'Father, your will be done.'

They are freed from evil thoughts, so that they cannot enter into them, no, not for a moment. Aforetime, when an evil thought came in, they looked up, and it vanished away. But now it does not come in, there being no room for this, in a soul which is full of God. They are free from wanderings in prayer. Whenever they pour out their hearts in a more immediate manner before God, they have no thought of any thing past [John Wesley's own footnote adds: 'This is far too strong.'], or absent, or to come, but of God alone. In times past, wandering thoughts darted in, which then fled away like smoke; but now that smoke does not rise at all. They have no fear or doubt, either as to their state in general, or as to any particular action. [John Wesley's footnote adds: 'Frequently this is the case; but only for a time.'] The anointing from the Holy One teaches them every hour what they shall do, and what they shall speak [John Wesley adds: 'For a time it may be so; but not always.']; nor therefore have they any need to reason concerning it. [John Wesley adds: 'Sometimes they have no need; at other times they have.']

They are in one sense freed from temptations; for though numberless temptations fly about them, yet

34

they do not trouble them. [John Wesley adds: 'Sometimes they do not; at other times they are oppressed by them.'] At all times their souls are even and calm, their hearts are steadfast and unmovable. Their peace, flowing as a river, 'transcends all understanding' (Phil. 4:7), and they 'are filled with an inexpressible and glorious joy' (1 Pet. 1:8). For they 'were marked in Christ with a seal, the promised Holy Spirit who is a deposit guaranteeing our inheritance until the redemption of those who are God's possession' (see Eph. 1:13–14). They have the witness in themselves that 'there is in store for them the crown of righteousness, which the Lord . . . will award . . . on that day' (see 2 Tim. 4:8). [John Wesley's footnote adds: 'Not all who are saved from sin; many of them have not attained it yet.']

'Not that everyone is a child of the devil, till he is thus renewed in love. On the contrary, whoever has a sure confidence in God, that, through the merits of Christ, his sins are forgiven, he is a child of God, and, if he abide in him, an heir of all the promises. Neither ought he in any way to throw away his trust, or to deny the faith he has received, because it is weak, or because it is 'refined by fire' (1 Pet. 1:7), so that his soul 'suffer grief in all kinds of trials' (1 Pet. 1:6).

Neither dare we affirm, as some have done, that all this salvation is given at once. There is indeed an instantaneous, as well as a gradual, work of God in his children, and we know there is no lack of a cloud of witnesses who have received, in one moment, either a clear sense of the forgiveness of their sins, or the abiding witness of the Holy Spirit. But we do not know a single instance, in any place, of a person's receiving in one and the same moment remission of sins, the abiding witness of the Spirit, and a new, a clean heart.

Indeed, how God may work we cannot tell, but the general manner wherein he does work is this. Those who once trusted in themselves that they were righteous, that they were rich, and increased in goods, and had need of nothing, are, by the Spirit of God applying his word, convinced that they are poor and naked (see Rev. 3:14–18).

All the things that they have done they remember, are brought to their remembrance and set in array before them, so that they see the wrath of God hanging over their heads, and feel that they deserve the damnation of hell. In their trouble they cry unto the Lord, and he shows them that he has taken away their sins, and opens the kingdom of heaven in their hearts, 'righteousness, peace and joy in the Holy Spirit' (Rom. 14:17). Sorrow and pain disappear, and 'sin is no longer their master' (see Rom. 6:14). Knowing they are justified freely through faith in his blood, they 'have peace with God through our Lord Jesus Christ' (Rom. 5:1), they 'rejoice in the hope of the glory of God' (Rom. 5:2), and 'God has poured out his love into their hearts' (see Rom. 5:5)

In this peace they remain for days, or weeks, or months, and commonly suppose they will not know war any more, till some of their old enemies, the cherished sins, or the sin which most easily beset them (perhaps anger or desire) attacks them again, and thrusts severely at them, so that they fall. Then arises fear, that they will not endure to the end; and often doubt whether God has not forgotten them, or whether they did not deceive themselves in thinking their sins were forgiven. Under these clouds, especially if they reason with the devil, they go about in a mourning all the day long. But it is seldom long before their Lord answers for himself, sending them the Holy Spirit to comfort them, to bear witness continually with their spirits that they are the children of God (see Rom. 8:12–16). Then they are indeed humble and gentle and teachable, even as a little child. And now first do they see the ground of their heart: [In 1765, Wesley added this footnote to this quote from his Preface: 'Is it not astonishing, that while this book is extant, which was published twenty-four years ago, anyone should assure me that this is a new doctrine, which I had never previously taught?'] which God before would not disclose to them, in case the soul should fail before him, and the spirit which he had made. Now they see all the hidden admonitions there, the depths of pride, self-will, and hell; yet having the witness in themselves, 'You are heirs – heirs of God and co-heirs with Christ, if indeed we share in his sufferings' (see Rom. 8:17), which continually heightens both the strong sense they then have of their inability to help themselves, and the inexpressible hunger they feel for a full renewal in his image, 'in true righteousness and holiness' (Eph. 4:24).

Then God is mindful of the desire of those that fear him, and gives them a good eye, and a pure heart. He stamps on them his own image and superscription, he recreates them in Christ Jesus, he comes to them with his Son and blessed Spirit and, fixing his abode in their souls, brings them to the 'Sabbath-rest that remains for the people of God' (see Heb. 4:9).

Here I cannot but remark,

1   That this is the strongest account we ever gave of Christian Perfection; indeed too strong in more than one particular.

2   That there is nothing which we have since added to the subject, either in verse or prose, which is not either directly or indirectly contained in this preface. So that whether our present doctrine is right or wrong, it is the same which we taught from the beginning.

Hymn from Hymns Volume II

I need not give additional proofs to this by multiplying quotations from the volume itself. It may suffice, to cite part of one hymn only, the last in that volume:

Lord, I believe a rest remains
To all thy people known;
A rest where pure enjoyment reigns,
And thou art loved alone.

A rest where all our soul's desire
Is fixed on things above;
Where doubt and pain and fear expire,
Cast out by perfect love.

From every evil motion freed
(The Son hath made us free),
On all the powers of hell we tread,
In glorious liberty.

Safe in the way of life, above
Death, earth, and hell we rise;
We find, when perfected in love,
Our long-sought paradise.

O that I now the rest might know,
Believe, and enter in!
Now, Saviour, now the power bestow,
And let me cease from sin!

Remove this hardness from my heart,
This unbelief remove;
To me the rest of faith impart,
The sabbath of thy love.

Come, O my Saviour, come away!
Into my soul descend;
No longer from thy creature stay,
My author and my end.

The bliss thou hast for me prepared
No longer be delay'd;
Come, my exceeding great reward,
For whom I first was made.

Come Father, Son and Holy Ghost,
And seal me thine abode!
Let all I am in thee be lost;
Let all be lost in God!

Can anything be more clear than,

1   That here also is as full and high a salvation as we have ever spoken of?

2   That this is being received by mere faith alone, and is hindered only by unbelief?

3   That this faith, and consequently the salvation it brings, is spoken of as being given in an instant?

4   That it is supposed that that instant may be now, and that we need not wait another moment; that actually, 'now is the time of God's favour, now is the day of' this full 'salvation' (see 2 Cor. 6:2).

5   And, lastly, if anyone speaks to the contrary, he is the person who brings new doctrine among us.

14   Third volume of Hymns, published in 1742

About a year later, that is in 1742, we published another volume of hymns. The dispute was now at its height and we spoke about this subject at greater length than ever before. Accordingly many of the hymns in this volume are explicitly on this subject, as is the Preface. Since this is short, it may not come amiss to quote it in full.

15   Preface to Charles and John Wesley's *Hymns* Volume III

1   Perhaps the general prejudice against Christian Perfection may chiefly arise from a misunderstanding about its nature. We willingly allow, and continually

declare, that there is no such thing as a perfection in this life, that implies either a dispensation from doing good, and observing all the ordinances of God, or a freedom from ignorance, mistake, temptation, and a thousand weaknesses which are necessarily connected with flesh and blood.

2   First. We not only allow, but earnestly contend, that there is no perfection in this life, which implies any dispensation from observing all the ordinances of God, or from doing good to all men while we have time, though 'especially to those who belong to the family of believers' (Gal. 6:10). We believe that not only the new-born babies in Christ, who have recently found redemption in his blood, but those also who are adult Christians, are indispensably obliged, as often as they have opportunity, to eat bread and drink wine in remembrance of him (see Luke 22:19), and 'diligently study the Scriptures' (John 5:39), by fasting, as well as temperance, to 'beat their bodies and make them their slave' (see 1 Cor. 9:27), and, above all, to pour out their souls in prayer, both secretly, and in the great congregation.

3   We secondly believe that there is no such thing as a perfection in this life that implies an entire deliverance either from ignorance or mistake in things not essential to salvation, or from numerous temptations, or from numberless weaknesses with which the corruptible body more or less presses down the soul. We cannot find any ground in scripture to suppose that any inhabitant of a house of clay is wholly exempt either from bodily infirmities, or from ignorance of many things, or to imagine that anyone is incapable of making a mistake, or of falling into various temptations.

4   But whom then do you mean by 'one that is perfect'? We mean one in whom is 'the mind which was in Christ,' and who so 'walks as Christ also walked'; a man 'who has clean hands and a pure heart' (Ps. 24:4), or who is 'purified from everything that contaminates body and spirit' (see 2 Cor. 7:1), one in whom 'there is

40

nothing to make his brother stumble' (see 1 John 2:10), and who, accordingly, 'cannot go on sinning' ['he cannot sin' AV] (1 John 3:9).

To explain this in a little more detail: we understand that the scriptural expression, 'become mature' ['a perfect man' AV] (Eph. 4:13), refers to the person in whom God has fulfilled his faithful word, 'you will be clean; I will cleanse you from all your impurities and from all your idols' (Ezek. 36:25). We understand from this one whom God has made holy throughout in body, soul, and spirit; one who 'walks in the light, as he is in the light, in whom there is no darkness at all; the blood of Jesus, his Son, having purified him from all sin' (see 1 John 1:7, 5)

5 This man can now testify to all mankind, 'I have been crucified with Christ and I no longer live, but Christ lives in me' (Gal. 2:20). He 'is holy as God who called him is holy' both in heart and 'in all he does' (see 1 Pet. 1:15–16). He 'loves the Lord his God with all his heart,' serves him 'with all his strength.' He 'loves his neighbour,' every man, 'as himself' (see Luke 10:27). Yes, 'as Christ loves us,' those people in particular, who curse him or persecute him, because they do not know the Son, or the one who sent him (see Luke 6:28; John 15:20–1). Indeed his soul is all love, filled with 'compassion, kindness, humility, gentleness and patience' (Col. 3:12). And his life agrees with this, being full of 'work produced by faith, labour prompted by love, and endurance inspired by hope' (see 1 Thess. 1:3). 'And whatever he does, whether in word or deed,' he does, 'it all in the name,' in the love and power, 'of the Lord Jesus' (see Col. 3:17). In a word, he does 'the will of God on earth, as it is done in heaven' (see Matt. 6:10).

6 This is what it is to be a perfect man, for God has 'made perfect for ever those who are being made holy' (Heb. 10:14), even 'to have a heart so all-flaming with the love of God' (to use Archbishop Usher's words) 'as continually to offer up every thought, word, and work,

as a spiritual sacrifice, acceptable to God through Jesus Christ' (see 1 Pet. 2:5). In every thought of our hearts, in every word of our tongues, in every work of our hands, to 'declare the praises of him who called you out of darkness into his wonderful light' (1 Pet. 2:9). Oh that both we, and all who seek the Lord Jesus in sincerity, may thus 'be brought to complete unity', ['be made perfect in one' AV] (John 17:23).

This is the doctrine which we preached from the beginning, and which we preach to this day. Indeed by scrutinising it from every angle, and comparing it again and again with the word of God on the one hand, and the experience of the children of God on the other, we saw further into the nature and properties of Christian Perfection. But still there is no conflict at all between our first and our last thoughts. Our first conception of Perfection was that it is to have 'the mind which was in Christ,' and to 'walk as he walked'; to have all the mind that was in him, and always to walk as he walked. In other words, to be inwardly and outwardly devoted to God; all devoted in heart and life. And we have the same conception of it now, without either adding anything or taking anything away.

16   Three hymns from *Hymns* Volume III

The hymns on this subject in this volume are too numerous to quote in full. I shall only quote from three of them:

> Saviour from sin, I wait to prove
> That Jesus is thy healing name;
> To lose, when perfected in love,
> Whate'er I have, or can, or am;
> I stay me on thy faithful word,
> 'The servant shall be as his Lord.'

Answer that gracious end in me
For which thy precious life was given;
Redeem from all iniquity,
Restore, and make me meet for heaven.
Unless thou purge my every stain,
Thy suffering and my faith are vain.

Didst thou not die, that I might live,
No longer to myself, but thee?
Might body, soul, and spirit give
To him who gave himself for me?
Come then, my Master, and my God,
Take the dear purchase of thy blood.

Thy own peculiar servant claim,
For thy own truth and mercy's sake;
Hallow in me thy glorious name;
Me for thine own this moment take,
And change and throughly purify;
Thine only may I live and die.

And

Choose from the world, if now I stand,
Adorn'd with righteousness divine;
If, brought into the promised land,
I justly call the Saviour mine;
The sanctifying Spirit pour,
To quench my thirst and wash me clean;
Now, Saviour, let the gracious shower
Descend, and make me pure from sin.

Purge me from every sinful blot;
My idols all be cast aside:
Cleanse me from every evil thought,
From all the filth of self and pride.
The hatred of the carnal mind
Out of my flesh at once remove:

Give me a tender heart, resign'd,
And pure, and full of faith and love.

O that I now, from sin released,
Thy word might to the utmost prove,
Enter into thy promised rest,
The Canaan of thy perfect love.

Now let me gain perfection's height!
Now let me into nothing fall,
Be less than nothing in my sight,
And feel that Christ is all in all.

Finally,

Lord, I believe, thy work of grace
Is perfect in the soul!
His heart is pure who sees thy face,
His spirit is made whole.

From every sickness, by thy word,
From every foul disease,
Saved, and to perfect health restored,
To perfect holiness.

He walks in glorious liberty,
To sin entirely dead;
The Truth, the Son hath made him free,
And he is free indeed.

Throughout his soul thy glories shine,
His soul is all renew'd,
And deck'd in righteousness divine,
And clothed and fill'd with God.

This is the rest, the life, the peace,
Which all thy people prove;
Love is the bond of perfectness,
And all their soul is love.

O joyful sound of gospel grace;
Christ shall in me appear;
I, even I, shall see his face,
I shall be holy here!

He visits now the house of clay,
He shakes his future home;
O wouldst thou, Lord, on this glad day,
Into thy temple come.

Come, O my God, thyself reveal,
Fill all this mighty void;
Thou only canst my spirit fill;
Come, O my God, my God!

Fulfil, fulfil my large desires,
Large as infinity;
Give, give me all my soul requires,
All, all that is in thee.

17 Summaries of the first four Methodist Conferences

On Monday, June 25th, 1744, our First Conference began; six clergymen and all our preachers being present. The next morning we seriously considered the doctrine of sanctification, or perfection. The questions asked about it, and the substance of the answers were as follows:

QUESTION   What is it to be sanctified?
ANSWER   To be renewed in the image of God, in true 'righteousness and holiness' (Eph. 4:24).
Q   What is implied in being a perfect Christian?
A   Love the Lord your God with all our heart, and with all your soul, and with all your strength' (Deut. 6:5).

Q   Does this imply, that all inward sin is taken away?
A   Undoubtedly; or how can we be said to be saved 'from all your uncleanness'? (Ezek. 36:29).

Our Second Conference began August 1st, 1745. The next morning we spoke about sanctification as follows:

Q   When does inward sanctification begin?
A   At the moment a man is justified. (Yet sin remains in him, yes, the seed of all sin, till he is sanctified throughout.) From that time a believer gradually dies to sin, and grows in grace.
Q   Is this usually given a little before death?
A   It is not, to those who expect it no sooner.
Q   But may we expect it sooner?
A   Why not? For, although we grant,
1   that most believers whom we have known up to now, were not so sanctified until near their deaths;
2   that few of those to whom St Paul wrote his Epistles were in that state at that time; nor,
3   he himself, at the time of writing his earlier letters; yet all this does not prove that we may not be so today.
Q   How should we preach about sanctification?
A   Hardly at all to those who are not pressing forward; but to those who are, always emphasising God's promise; always drawing, rather than driving.

Our Third Conference began Tuesday, May 26th, 1746.
In this we carefully read over the minutes of the two preceding conferences, to observe whether anything contained in them might be withdrawn or altered on more mature consideration. But we did not see any cause to alter in any respect what we had agreed upon before.
Our Fourth Conference began on Tuesday, June 16th, 1747. As several people were present who did not believe in the doctrine of Perfection, we agreed to examine it from the foundation.

In order to do this, it was asked,

Q How much is conceded by our brethren, who differ from us, with regard to entire sanctification?
A They grant,
1 That everyone must be entirely sanctified at the moment of death.
2 That until then a believer daily grows in grace and comes nearer and nearer to perfection.
3 That we ought to be continually pressing after it, and to exhort all others so to do.
Q What do we concede to them?
A We grant,
1 That many of those who have died in the faith, yes, the majority of the people we have known, were not perfected in love, until a little before their death.
2 That the term *sanctified*, is always applied by St Paul to all who were justified.
3 That by this term alone it rarely, if ever, means, 'saved from all sin'.
4 That, consequently, it is not proper to use it in that sense, without adding the words *wholly, entirely*, or the like.
5 That the inspired writers almost always speak about or to those who were justified, but very rarely about or to those who were wholly sanctified. [John Wesley added this footnote: 'That is, unto those alone, exclusive of others; but they speak to them jointly with others, almost always.']
6 That, consequently, we must almost always speak of the state of justification; but more rarely. [John Wesley adds this footnote: 'More rarely, I allow; but yet in some places very frequently, strongly and explicitly.']
Q What then is the point where we divide?
A It is this: Should we expect to be saved from all sin before the moment of death?
Q Is there any clear scripture promise of this – that

God will save us from all sin?

A There is: 'He himself will redeem Israel from all their sins' (Ps. 130:8). This is expressed in more detail in the prophecy of Ezekiel: 'I will sprinkle clean water on you, and you will be clean; I will cleanse you from all your impurities and from all your idols . . . I will save you from all your uncleanness' (Ezek. 36:25, 29). No promise can be more clear. And the apostle plainly refers to this in his exortation: 'Since we have these promises, dear friends, let us purify ourselves from everything that contaminates body and spirit, perfecting holiness out of reverence for God' (2 Cor. 7:1). Equally clear and explicit is that ancient promise: 'The Lord your God will circumcise your hearts and the hearts of your descendants, so that you may love him with all your heart and with all your soul, and life' (Deut. 30:6).

Q But is there any corroboration of this in the New Testament?

A There is, and the New Testament sets it out very clearly. It is seen in 1 John 3:8: 'The reason the Son of God appeared was to destroy the devil's work;' the works of the devil, without any limitation or restriction; but all sin is the work of the devil. Parallel to which is the assertion of St Paul: 'Christ loved the church and gave himself up for her to make her holy . . . to present her to himself as a radiant church, without stain or wrinkle or any other blemish' (Eph. 5:25–7) And to the same effect is his assertion in Romans 8:3–4. 'For what the law was powerless to do in that it was weakened by the sinful nature, God did by sending his own Son . . . in order that the righteous requirements of the law might be fully met in us, who do not live according to the sinful nature but according to the Spirit.'

Q Does the New Testament afford any farther ground for expecting to be saved from all sin?

A Undoubtedly it does; both in those prayers and commands, which are equivalent to the strongest assertions.

48

Q   What prayers do you mean?
A   Prayers for entire sanctification; which, if there
was no such thing, would be just mocking God. In particular,
1   'Deliver us from the evil one' (Matt. 6:13). Now,
when this is done, when we are delivered from all evil,
there can be no sin remaining.
2   My prayer is not for them alone. I pray also for
those who will believe in me through their message,
that all of them may be one, Father, just as you are in
me and I am in you. May they also be in us so that the
world may believe that you have sent me. I have given
them the glory that you gave me, that they may be one
as we are one: 'I in them and you in me. May they be
brought to complete unity' ['I in them and thou in me,
that they may be made perfect in one'] (John 17:23,
AV).
3   'For this reason I kneel before the Father . . . And
I pray that you, being rooted and established in love,
may have power, together with all the saints, to grasp
how wide and long and high and deep is the love of
Christ, and to know this love that surpasses knowledge
– that you may be filled to the measure of all the fulness
of God' (Eph. 3:14, 17–19).
4   'May God himself, the God of peace, sanctify you
through and through. May your whole spirit, soul and
body be kept blameless at the coming of our Lord Jesus
Christ' (1 Thess. 5:23).
Q   What command is there to the same effect?
A   1   'Be perfect, therefore, as your heavenly Father
is perfect' (Matt. 5:48).
2   'Love the Lord your God with all your heart and
with all your soul and with all your mind' (Matt. 22:37).
But if the love of God fill the heart, there can be no sin
therein.
Q   But how will this happen before the moment of
death?
A   1   From the very nature of a command, which is

not given to the dead, but to the living. Therefore, 'Love the Lord your God with all your heart', cannot mean, You will do this when you die, but, while you live.

2   From the explicit texts of scripture:

i   'For the grace of God that brings salvation has appeared to all men. It teaches us to say "No" to ungodliness and worldly passions, and to live self-controlled, upright and godly lives in this present age, while we wait for the blessed hope – the glorious appearing of our great God and Saviour, Jesus Christ, who gave himself for us to redeem us from all wickedness and to purify for himself a people that are his very own, eager to do what is good' (Titus 2:11–14).

ii   'He has raised up a horn of salvation for us . . . to show mercy to our fathers . . . the oath he swore to our father Abraham: to rescue us from the hand of our enemies, and to enable us to serve him without fear in holiness and righteousness before him all our days' (Luke 1:69, 72–5).

Q   Is there any example in scripture of persons who had attained this?

A   Yes; St John, and all those of whom he says, in this way, 'Love is made complete among us so that we will have confidence on the day of judgment, because in this world we are like him' (1 John 4:17). ['Herein is our love made perfect, that we may have boldness in the day of judgment: because as he is, so are we in this world' (AV).]

Q   Can you show one such example? Where is he that is thus perfect?

A   To some who make this inquiry one might answer, 'If I knew one here, I would not tell you; for you do not inquire out of love. You are like Herod; you only seek the young child in order to kill it.' But more directly we answer: There are many reasons why there should be few, if any, indisputable examples. What an inconvenience would this bring on the person himself, set as a mark for all to shoot at! And how unprofitable it would be to those who contradict him! 'If they do not listen to Moses and the Prophets,' Christ and his apostles, 'they will not be convinced even if someone rises from the dead' (Luke 16:31).

Q   Are we not apt to have a secret dislike of any who say that they are saved from all sin?

A   It is very possible we may, and that upon several grounds; partly from a concern for the good of souls, who may be hurt if these are not what they profess; partly from a kind of implicit envy at those who speak of higher attainments than our own; and partly from our natural slowness and unreadiness of heart to believe the works of God.

Q   Why may we not continue in the joy of faith till we are perfected in love?

A   Why indeed? Since holy grief does not quench this joy; since even while we are under the cross, while we deeply partake of the sufferings of Christ, we may rejoice with inexpressible joy.

From these extracts it is totally clear not only what my brother and I believed but also what was the judgment of all the preachers linked to us from 1744 to 1747. I do not remember a single dissenting voice from these Conferences. Whatever doubts any one had when we met, they were all removed before we parted.

18   Hymns from *Hymns and Sacred Poems* Volumes I and II

In 1749, my brother published two volumes of *Hymns and Sacred Poems*. As I did not see these before they were printed, there were some things in them which I did not approve of. But I fully approved the main point of the hymns; a few verses from these hymns now follow:

Come, Lord, be manifested here,
And all the devil's works destroy;
Now, without sin, in me appear,
And fill with everlasting joy:
Thy beatific face display;
Thy presence is the perfect day.

                    (Vol. I, p. 203.)

Swift to my rescue come,
Thy own this moment seize;
Gather my wand'ring spirit home,
And keep in perfect peace.

Suffer'd no more to rove
O'er all the earth abroad,
Arrest the pris'ner to thy love,
And shut me up in God!

                    (Vol. I, p. 247.)

Thy pris'ners release, Vouchsafe us thy peace;
And our sorrows and sins in a moment shall cease.
That moment be now! Our petition allow,
Our present Redeemer and Comforter thou!

                    (Vol. II, p.124.)

From this inbred sin deliver;
Let the yoke Now be broke;
Make me thine for ever.

Partner of thy perfect nature,
Let me be Now in thee
A new, sinless creature.

                    (Vol. II, p. 156.)

Turn me, Lord, and turn me now,
To thy yoke my spirit bow:

Grant me now the pearl to find
Of a meek and quiet mind.

Calm, O calm my troubled breast;
Let me gain that second rest:
From my works for ever cease,
Perfected in holiness.

(Vol. II, p. 162.)

Come in this accepted hour,
Bring thy heavenly kingdom in!
Fill us with the glorious power,
Rooting out the seeds of sin.

(Vol. II, p. 168.)

Come, thou dear Lamb, for sinners slain,
Bring in the cleansing flood:
Apply, to wash out every stain,
Thine efficacious blood.

O let it sink into our soul
Deep as the inbred sin:
Make every wounded spirit whole,
And every leper clean!

(Vol. II, p. 171.)

Pris'ners of hope, arise,
And see your Lord appear:
Lo! on the wings of love he flies,
And brings redemption near.

Redemption in his blood
He calls you to receive:
'Come unto me, the pard'ning God:
Believe,' he cries, 'believe!'

Jesus, to thee we look,
Till saved from sin's remains,

Reject the inbred tyrant's yoke,
And cast away his chains.

Our nature shall no more
O'er us dominion have:
By faith we apprehend the power,
Which shall for ever save.

(Vol. II, p. 188.)

Jesu, our life, in us appear,
Who daily die thy death:
Reveal thyself the finisher;
Thy quick'ning Spirit breathe!

Unfold the hidden mystery,
The second gift impart;
Reveal thy glorious self in me,
In every waiting heart.

(Vol. II, p. 195.)

In him we have peace, In him we have power!
Preserved by his grace Throughout the dark hour.
In all our temptations He keeps us, to prove
His utmost salvation, His fullness of love.

Pronounce the glad word, And bid us be free!
Ah, hast thou not, Lord, A blessing for me?
The peace thou hast given, This moment impart,
And open thy heaven, O Love, in my heart!

(Vol. II, p. 324.)

A second edition of these hymns was published in 1752, which had no alterations, other than a few literals.

In these extracts I have expanded on this subject because it becomes clear beyond any possibility of contradiction what my brother and I have maintained to this day:

1 That Christian Perfection is that love of God and our neighbour, which implies deliverance from all sin.
2 That this is received by faith alone.
3 That it is given instantaneously, in one moment.
4 That we are to expect it, not at death, but every moment; that now is the accepted time, now is the day of this salvation.

19 *Thoughts on Christian Perfection*

At the Conference in 1759, perceiving some danger that a diversity of thinking should imperceptibly take a hold on us, we again considered this doctrine in detail. Soon after this I published *Thoughts on Christian Perfection*, prefaced with the following advertisement:

The following tract is by no means designed to gratify the curiosity of any man. It is not intended to prove the doctrine at large, in opposition to those who explode and ridicule it; no, nor to answer the numerous objections against it, which may be raised even by serious men. All I intend here is simply to declare what are my sentiments on the main point; what Christian Perfection does, according to my apprehension, include, and what it does not; and to add a few practical observations and directions relative to the subject.

As these thoughts were at first thrown together by way of question and answer, I let them continue in the same form. They are just the same that I have entertained for above twenty years.

QUESTION What is Christian Perfection?
ANSWER The loving of God with all our heart, mind, soul, and strength. This implies, that no wrong frame of mind, nothing contrary to love, remains in the soul; and that all the thoughts, words and actions,

are governed by pure love.

Q Do you affirm that this perfection excludes all infirmities, ignorance and mistakes?

A I continually affirm quite the opposite, and have always done so.

Q But how can every thought, word and work, be governed by pure love, and the man be subject at the same time to ignorance and mistake?

A I see no contradiction here: 'A man may be filled with pure love, and still be liable to mistake.' Indeed I do not expect to be freed from actual mistakes till this mortal puts on immortality. I believe this to be a natural consequence of the soul's dwelling in flesh and blood. For we cannot now think at all, but by the mediation of those bodily organs which have suffered equally with the rest of our frame. And hence we cannot avoid sometimes thinking wrong, till this corruptible shall have put on incorruption.

But we may carry this thought farther yet. A mistake in judgment may possibly occasion a mistake in practice. (For instance: Mr De Renty's mistake touching the nature of mortification, arising from prejudice of education, occasioned that practical mistake, his wearing an iron girdle.) And a thousand such instances there may be, even in those who are in the highest state of grace. Yet, where every word and action spring from love, such a mistake is not properly a sin. However, it cannot bear the rigour of God's justice, but needs the atoning blood.

Q What was the judgment of all our brethren who met at Bristol in August 1758, on this subject?

A It was expressed in these words:

1 Every one may make mistakes as long as he lives.

2 A mistake in thinking may occasion a mistake in practice.

3 Every such mistake is a transgression of the perfect law. Therefore,

4 Every such mistake, were it not for the blood of

atonement, would expose to eternal damnation.

5   It follows that the most perfect have continual need of the merits of Christ, even for their actual transgressions, and may say for themselves, as well as for their brethren, 'Forgive us our sins.'

This easily accounts for what might otherwise seem to be utterly unaccountable; namely, that those who are not offended when we speak of the highest degree of love, yet will not hear of living without sin. The reason is, they know all men are liable to mistakes, and that in practice as well as in thinking. But they do not know, or do not observe, that this is not so, if love is the sole principle of action.

Q   But still, if they live without sin, does not this exclude the necessity of a Mediator? At least, is it not plain that they stand no longer in need of Christ in his priestly office?

A   Far from it. None feels their need of Christ like these; none so entirely depend upon him. For Christ does not give life to the soul separate from, but in and with himself. Hence his words are equally true of all men, in whatsoever state of grace they are: 'No branch can bear fruit by itself; it must remain in the vine. Neither can you bear fruit unless you remain in me . . . apart from me [or separate from] you can do nothing' (John 15:4–5).

In every state we need Christ in the following respects:

1   Whatever grace we receive, it is a free gift from him.

2   We receive it as his purchase, merely in consideration of the price he paid.

3   We have this grace, not only from Christ, but in him. For our perfection is not like that of a tree, which flourishes by the sap derived from its own root, but, as was said before, like that of a branch which, united to the vine, bears fruit; but, severed from it, is dried up and withered.

4   All our blessings, temporal, spiritual and eternal,

depend on his intercession for us, which is one branch of his priestly office, whereof therefore we have always equal need.

5 The best of men still need Christ in his priestly office, to atone for their omissions, their short-comings, (as some not improperly speak), their mistakes in thinking and practice, and their defects of various kinds. For these are all deviations from the perfect law, and consequently need an atonement. Yet that they are not really sins, we apprehend may appear from the words of St Paul, 'He who loves his fellow-man has fulfilled the law . . . Therefore love is the fulfilment of the law' (Rom. 13:8, 10). Now, mistakes, and whatever infirmities necessarily flow from the corruptible state of the body, are in no way contrary to love; nor therefore, in the scriptural sense, sin.

To explain myself a little more on this subject:

1 Not only sin, properly so called (that is, a voluntary transgression of a known law), but sin, incorrectly so called (that is, an involuntary transgression of a divine law, known or unknown), needs the atoning blood.

2 I believe there is no such perfection in this life as excludes these involuntary transgressions which I apprehend to be naturally consequent on the ignorance and mistakes inseparable from mortality.

3 Therefore *sinless perfection* is a phrase I never use, lest I should seem to contradict myself.

4 I believe a person filled with love of God is still liable to these involuntary transgressions.

5 Such transgressions you may call sins, if you please: I do not, for these reasons above-mentioned.

Q What advice would you give to those that do, and those that do not, call them so?

A Let those that do not call them sins, never think that themselves or any other persons are in such a state as that they can stand before infinite justice without a Mediator. This must argue either the deepest ignorance, or the highest arrogance and presumption.

Let those who do call them so, beware how they confound these defects with sins, properly so called.

But how will they avoid it? How will these be distinguished from those, if they are all indiscriminately called sins? I am much afraid, if we should allow my sins to be consistent with perfection, few would confine the idea to those defects concerning which only the assertion could be true.

Q But how can a tendency to making mistakes coexist with perfect love? Is not a person who is perfected in love every moment under its influence? And can any mistake flow from pure love?

A I answer,

1 Many mistakes may coexist with pure love;

2 Some may accidentally flow from it: I mean, love itself may incline us to mistake. The pure love of our neighbour, springing from the love of God, thinks no evil, believes and hopes all things. Now, this very frame of mind, unsuspicious, ready to believe and hope the best of all men, may sometimes make us think some men are better than they really are. Here then is a clear mistake, accidentally flowing from pure love.

Q How shall we avoid setting perfection too high or too low?

A By keeping to the Bible, and setting it just as high as the scripture does. It is nothing higher and nothing lower than this – the pure love of God and man; the loving of God with all our heart and soul, and our neighbour as ourselves. It is love governing the heart and life, running through our whole mentality, words, and actions.

Q Suppose one had attained to this, would you advise him to speak of it?

A At first, perhaps, he would scarce be able to refrain, the fire would be so hot within him; his desire to declare the loving-kindness of the Lord carrying him away like a torrent. But afterwards he might; and then it would be advisable, not to speak of it to those who do not know God (it is most likely, it would only provoke them to contradict and blaspheme); nor to others, without some particular reason, without some good in view. And to them he should have special care to avoid all appearance of boasting; to speak with the deepest humility and reverence, giving all the glory to God.

Q   But would it not be better to be entirely silent, not to speak of it at all?

A   By silence, he might avoid many crosses, which will naturally and necessarily ensue, if he simply declare, even among believers, what God has wrought in his soul. If, therefore, such a one were to confer with flesh and blood, he would be entirely silent. But this could not be done with a clear conscience; for undoubtedly he ought to speak. Men do not light a candle to put it under a bowl; much less does the all-wise God. He does not raise such a monument of his power and love to hide it from all mankind. Rather, he intends it as a general blessing to those who are simple of heart. He designs thereby not barely the happiness of that individual person but to animate and encourage others to follow after the same blessing. His will is, 'that many shall see it' and rejoice, 'and put their trust in the Lord.' Nor does anything under heaven more enliven the desires of those who are justified, than to converse with those whom they believe to have experienced a still higher salvation. This places salvation full in their view, and increases their hunger and thirst after it; an advantage which must have been entirely lost, had the person so saved buried himself in silence.

Q   But is there no way to prevent these crosses which usually fall on those who speak of being thus saved?

A   It seems they cannot be prevented altogether, while so much of nature remains even in believers. But something might be done, if the preacher in every place would,

1   Talk freely with all who speak thus; and,

2   labour to prevent the unjust or unkind treatment

of those in favour of whom there is reasonable proof.

Q   What is reasonable proof? How may we certainly know one that is saved from all sin?

A   We cannot infallibly know one that is thus saved (no, nor even one that is justified), unless it should please God to endow us with the miraculous discernment of spirits. But we understand that those would be sufficient proofs to any reasonable man, and such as would leave little room to doubt either the truth or depth of the work:

1   If we had clear evidence of his exemplary behaviour for some time before this supposed change, this would give us reason to believe he would not 'lie for God', but speak neither more nor less than he felt;

2   if he gave a distinct account of the time and manner wherein the change came about, with sound speech which could not be reproved; and,

3   if it appeared that all his subsequent words and actions were holy and unblamable.

The matter can be summarised like this:

1   I have abundant reason to believe this person will not lie;

2   he testifies before God, 'I feel no sin, but all love; I pray, rejoice and give thanks without ceasing; and I have as clear an inward witness that I am fully renewed as that I am justified.' Now, if I have nothing to oppose to this plain testimony, I ought in reason to believe it.

It avails nothing to object, 'But I know several things wherein he is quite mistaken.' For it has been allowed that all who are in the body are liable to make mistakes; and that a mistake in reasoning may sometimes cause a mistake to be made in practice; though great care is to be taken that no ill use is made of this concession. For instance: Even one who is perfected in love may make a mistake with regard to another person, and may think him, in a particular case, to be more or less faulty than he really is. And hence he may speak to him with more or less severity than the truth requires. And in this sense (though that be not the primary meaning of St James), 'whoever keeps the whole law and yet stumbles at just one point is guilty of breaking all of it' (Jas. 2:10). This therefore is no proof at all that the person so speaking is not perfect.

Q   But is it not a proof, if he is surprised or thrown into confusion by a noise, a fall, or some sudden danger?

A   It is not; for one may jump, tremble, change colour, or be otherwise disordered in body, while the soul is calmly stayed on God, and remains in perfect peace. No, the mind itself may be deeply distressed, may be exceeding sorrowful, may be perplexed and pressed down by heaviness and anguish, even to agony, while the heart clings to God by perfect love, and the will is wholly resigned to him. Was it not so with the Son of God himself? Does any child of man endure the distress, the anguish, the agony, which he sustained? And yet he knew no sin.

Q   But can any one who has a pure heart prefer pleasing to unpleasing food; or use any pleasure of sense which is not strictly necessary? If so, how do they differ from others?

A   The difference between those and others in taking pleasant food is,

1   They need none of these things to make them happy; for they have a spring of happiness within. They see and love God. Hence they rejoice evermore, and in everything give thanks.

2   They may use them, but they do not seek them.

3   They use them sparingly, and not for the sake of the thing itself. This being premised, we answer directly. Such a one may use pleasing food, without the danger which attends those who are not saved from sin. He may prefer it to unpleasing, though equally wholesome, food, as a means of increasing thankfulness, with a single eye to God, who richly provides us everything for our enjoyment (1 Tim. 6:17). On the

same principle, he may smell a flower, or eat a bunch of grapes, or take any other pleasure which does not lessen but increase his delight in God. Therefore, neither can we say that one perfected in love would be incapable of marriage, and of worldly business. If he were called thereto, he would be more capable than ever, as being able to do all things without hurry or carefulness, without any distraction of spirit.

Q   But if two perfect Christians had children, how could they be born in sin, since there was none in the parents?

A   It is a possible, but not a probable, case. I doubt whether it ever was or ever will be. But waiving this, I answer, Sin is imposed upon me, not by my human parents, but by my first parent. '. . . In Adam all die . . . through the disobedience of one man the many were made sinners' (1 Cor. 15:22; Rom. 5:19). All men, without exception, who were in his body when he ate the forbidden fruit.

We have a remarkable illustration of this in gardening. Grafts on a crab-stock bear excellent fruit, but sow the seeds of this fruit, and what will be the result? They produce the purest crabs as ever were eaten.

Q   But what does the perfect one do more than others? More than the common believers?

A   Perhaps nothing; so may the providence of God have hedged him in by outward circumstances. Perhaps not so much; though he desires and longs to spend and be spent for God; at least, not externally. He neither speaks so many words, nor does so many works. As neither did our Lord himself speak so many works, or do so many, no, nor so great deeds, as some of his apostles (John 14:12). But what does this mean then? This is no proof that he has not more grace; and by this God measures the outward work. Listen to him: 'this poor widow has put more into the treasury than all the others' (Mark 12:43). Truly, this poor man, with his few broken words, has spoken more than them all.

Truly, this poor woman, that has given a cup of cold water, has done more than them all. 'Stop judging by mere appearances', and learn to 'make a right judgment' (John 7:24).

Q   But is not this a proof against him – I feel no power either in his words or prayer?

A   It is not; for perhaps that is your own fault. You are not likely to feel any power therein, if any of these hindrances lie in the way:

1   Your own deadness of soul. The dead Pharisees felt no power even in Jesus's words, about which the guards declared, 'No-one ever spoke the way this man does' (John 7:46).

2   The guilt of some unrepented sin lying upon the conscience.

3   Prejudice towards him of any kind.

4   Your not believing that state to be attainable wherein he professes to be.

5   Unreadiness to think or acknowledge he has attained it.

6   Overvaluing or idolising him.

7   Overvaluing yourself and your own judgment.

If any of these is the case, what wonder is it that you feel no power in anything he says? But do not others feel it? If they do, your argument falls to the ground. And if they do not, do none of these hindrances lie in their way, too? You must be certain of this before you can build any argument thereon; and even then your argument will prove no more than that grace and gifts do not always go together.

Q   But what if he does not come up to my idea of a perfect Christian?

A   And perhaps no one ever did, or ever will. For your idea may go beyond, or at least beside, the scriptural account. It may include more than the Bible includes therein, or, however, something which it does not include. Scriptural perfection is pure love filling the heart and governing all the words and actions. If your idea includes anything more or anything else, it is not scriptural; and then no wonder that a scripturally perfect Christian does not come up to it.

I fear many stumble on this stumbling-block. They include as many ingredients as they please, not according to scripture, but according to their own imagination, in their idea of one that is perfect; and then readily deny any one to be such, who does not answer that imaginary idea.

The more care should we take to keep the simple, scriptural account continually in view. Pure love reigning alone in the heart and life – this then is the whole of scriptural perfection.

Q   When may a person judge himself to have attained this?

A   When, after having been fully convinced of inbred sin, by a far deeper and clearer conviction than that he experienced before justification, and after having experienced a gradual mortification of it, he experiences a total death to sin, and an entire renewal in the love and image of God, so as to rejoice evermore, to pray continually, and give thanks in every situation (1 Thess. 5:17–18). Not that 'to feel all love and no sin' is sufficient proof. Several have experienced this for a time, before their souls were fully renewed. None therefore ought to believe that the work is done, till there is added the testimony of the Spirit, witnessing his entire sanctification, as clearly as his justification.

Q   But why is it, that some people imagine they are thus sanctified, when in reality they are not?

A   It is hence; they do not judge by all the preceding marks, but either by part of them, or by others that are ambiguous. But I know no instance of a person's attending to them all, and yet deceived in this matter. I believe there can be none in the world. If a man be deeply and fully convinced, after justification, of inbred sin; if he then experiences a gradual mortification of sin, and afterwards an entire renewal in the image of God; if to this change, immensely greater than that wrought when he was justified, be added a clear, direct witness of the renewal; I judge it is impossible this man should be deceived herein, as that God should lie. And if one whom I know to be a man of veracity testifies these things to me, I ought not without some sufficient reason to reject his testimony.

Q   Is this death to sin, and renewal in love, gradual or instantaneous?

A   A man may be dying for some time; yet he does not, properly speaking, die till the instant the soul is separated from the body; and in that instant he lives the life of eternity. In the same way, he may be dying to sin for some time; yet he is not dead to sin, till sin is separated from his soul; and in that instant he lives the full life of love. And as the change undergone, when the body dies, is of a different kind, and infinitely greater than any we had known before, yes, such as till then it is impossible to conceive; so the change made, when the soul dies to sin, is of a different kind, and infinitely greater than any before, and than any can conceive till he experiences it. Yet he still grows in grace, in the knowledge of Christ, in the love and image of God; and will do so, not only till death, but to all eternity.

Q   How are we to wait for this change?

A   Not in careless indifference, or indolent inactivity; but in vigorous, universal obedience, in a zealous keeping of all the commandments, in watchfulness and diligence, in dying to ourselves, and in taking up our cross daily; as well as in earnest prayer and fasting, and a close attendance on all the ordinances of God. And if any man dream of attaining it any other way (yes, or of keeping it when it is attained, when he has received it even in the largest measure), he deceives his own soul. It is true, we receive it by simple faith. But God does not, will not, give that faith, unless we seek it with all diligence, in the way in which he has ordained.

This consideration may satisfy those who enquire, why so few have received the blessing. Enquire how many are seeking it in this way, and you have a sufficient answer.

Prayer especially is lacking. Who continues faithful therein? Who wrestles with God for this very thing? So, 'you do not receive, because you ask with wrong motives' (Jas. 4:3), namely, that you may be renewed before you die. *Before you die!* Will you be content with that? No, but ask that it may be done now; today, while it is called today. Do not call this 'setting God a time.' Certainly, today is his time as well as tomorrow. Hurry, man, hurry! Let

> Thy soul break out in strong desire
> The perfect bliss to prove;
> Thy longing heart be all on fire
> To be dissolved in love!

Q   But may we not continue in peace and joy till we are perfect in love?
A   Certainly we may; for the kingdom of God is not divided against itself; therefore, let not believers be discouraged from 'Rejoicing in the Lord always' (see Phil. 4:4). And yet our senses may be pained by the sinful nature that still remains in us. It is good for us to have a piercing sense of this, and a vehement desire to be delivered from it. But this should only encourage us the more earnestly to 'press on towards the goal to win the prize for which God has called us heavenward in Christ Jesus' (see Phil. 3:14). And when the sense of our sin most abounds, the sense of his love should much more abound.
Q   How should we treat those who think they have attained?
A   Examine them candidly, and exhort them to pray fervently, that God would show them all that is in their hearts. The most earnest exhortations to abound in

every grace, and the strongest cautions to avoid all evil, are given throughout the New Testament, to those who are in the highest state of grace. But this should be done with the utmost tenderness; and without any harshness, sternness, or sourness. We should carefully avoid the very appearance of anger, unkindness, or contempt. Leave it to Satan thus to tempt, and to his children to cry out, 'Let us examine him with despitefulness and torture, that we may know his meekness and prove his patience.' If they are faithful to the grace given, they are in no danger of perishing thereby; no, not if they remain in that error till their spirit is returning to God.

Q But what hurt can it do to deal harshly with them?

A Either they are mistaken, or they are not. If they are, it may destroy their souls. This is nothing impossible, no, nor improbable. It may so enrage or so discourage them that they will sink and rise no more. If they are not mistaken, it may grieve those whom God has not grieved, and do much hurt to our own souls. For undoubtedly he who touches them, touches, as it were, the apple of God's eye. If they are indeed full of his Spirit, to behave unkindly or contemptuously to them is doing no little contempt to the Spirit of grace. In this, likewise, we feed and increase in ourselves evil surmising and many wrong attitudes. To instance only one: What self-sufficiency is this, to set ourselves up as general inquisitors, as peremptory judges in the deep things of God! Are we qualified for the office? Can we pronounce, in all cases, how far weakness reaches? What may, and what may not, be resolved into it? What may in all circumstances, and what may not, exist with perfect love? Can we precisely determine, how it will influence the look, the gesture, the tone of voice? If we can, 'Doubtless we are the people, and wisdom will die with us' (see Job 12:2).

Q But if they are displeased at our not believing them, is not this definite proof against them?

A It depends on the nature of that displeasure: If they are angry, it is a proof against them; if they are grieved, it is not. They ought to be grieved, if we disbelieve a real work of God, and thereby deprive ourselves of the advantage we might have received from it. And we may easily mistake this grief for anger, as the outward expressions of both are much alike.

Q But is it not well to find out those who fancy they have attained when they have not?

A It is well to do it by mild, loving examination. But it is not well to triumph even over these. It is extremely wrong, if we find such an instance, to rejoice as if we had found great spoils. Ought we not rather to grieve, to be deeply concerned, to let our eyes run down with tears? Here is one who seemed to be a living proof of God's power to save completely (see Heb. 7:25); but, alas, it is not as we hoped. He is 'weighed on the scales and found wanting' (Dan. 5:27)! And is this a matter of joy? Ought we not to rejoice a thousand times more if we can find nothing but pure love?

'But he is deceived.' What follows from this? It is a harmless mistake, while he feels nothing but love in his heart. It is a mistake which generally argues great grace, a high degree both of holiness and happiness. This should be a matter of real joy to all that are simple of heart; not the mistake itself, but the height of grace which for a time occasions it. I rejoice that this soul is always happy in Christ, always full of prayer and thanksgiving. I rejoice that he feels no unholy emotion, but the pure love of God continually. And I will rejoice, if sin is suspended till it is totally destroyed.

Q Is there no danger that a man is being thus deceived?

A Not at the time that he feels no sin. There was danger before, and there will be again when he comes into fresh trials. But so long as he feels nothing but love animating all his thoughts and words and actions, he is in no danger; he is not only happy, but safe, 'in the shadow of the Almighty' (Ps. 91:1); and, for God's sake, let him continue in that love as long as he can. Meantime, you may do well to warn him of the danger that comes, if his love grows cold and sin revives; even the danger of casting away hope, and supposing that because he has not attained yet, therefore he never will.

Q   But what if none has attained it yet? What if all who think so are deceived?

A   Convince me of this, and I will preach it no more. But understand me right: I do not build any doctrine on this or that person. This or any other man may be deceived, and I am not moved. But, if there is none made perfect yet, God has not sent me to preach perfection.

Put a parallel case: for many years I have preached, 'The peace of God transcends all understanding' (see Phil. 4:7). Convince me that this word has fallen to the ground; that in all these years none has attained this peace; that there is no living witness of it at this day; and I will preach it no more.

'O, but several persons have died in that peace.' Perhaps so, but I want living witnesses. I cannot indeed be infallibly certain that this or that person is a witness; but if I were certain there is none such, I must finish with this doctrine.

'You misunderstand me. I believe some who died in this love, enjoyed it long before their death. But I was not certain that their former testimony was true till some hours before they died.'

You had not an infallible certainty then: and a reasonable certainty you might have had before; such a certainty as might have enlivened and comforted your own soul, and answered all other Christian purposes. Such a certainty as this any candid person may have, suppose there be any living witness, by talking one hour with that person in the love and fear of God.

Q   But what does it signify, whether any have

70

attained it or not, seeing so many scriptures bear witness to it?

A   If I were convinced that none in England had attained what has been so clearly and strongly preached by such a number of preachers, in so many places, and for so long a time, I should be clearly convinced that we had all mistaken the meaning of those scriptures; and therefore, for the time to come, I too must teach that 'sin will remain until death.'

20   God's work in London in 1762

In 1762, God's work greatly increased in London. Many, who had until then cared nothing for these things, were deeply convinced about their lost condition; many found redemption in the blood of Christ; not a few backsliders were healed; and a considerable number of people believed that God had saved them from all sin. Because it was easy to predict that Satan would try to sow tares among the wheat, I took great pains to warn them of the danger, particularly about pride and enthusiasm. And while I stayed in town, I had reason to hope they continued both humble and sober-minded. But almost as soon as I was gone enthusiasm broke in. Two or three began to substitute their own imaginations for visions from God, and from there to suppose they should never die; and these, working hard to bring others into the same opinion, brought about much noise and confusion. Soon after, the same people, with a few others, fell into more extreme ideas; claiming that they could not be tempted; that they could feel no more pain; and that they had the gift of prophecy, and of distinguishing between spirits. On my return to London in the autumn, some of them stood reproved; but others had risen above instruction. Meantime, a flood of reproach came upon me from almost every quarter; from themselves, because I was checking them all the time; and from others because, they said, I did not check them. However, the hand of the Lord was not stayed, but more and more sinners were convinced; while some were converted to God nearly every day, and others were enabled to love him with all their hearts.

21   Letter from a friend

At about this time, a friend who lived some distance from London wrote me the following letter:

Be not over alarmed that Satan sows tares among the wheat of Christ. It ever has been so, especially on any remarkable outpouring of his Spirit; and ever will be so, till Satan is chained up for a thousand years. Till then he will always ape, and endeavour to counteract, the work of the Spirit of Christ.

One melancholy effect of this has been that a world, who is always asleep in the arms of the evil one, has ridiculed every work of the Holy Spirit.

But what can real Christians do? Why, if they would act worthy of themselves, they should,

1   Pray that every deluded soul may be delivered;

2   endeavour to reclaim them in the spirit of meekness; and,

3   lastly, take the utmost care, both by prayer and watchfulness, that the delusion of others may not lessen their zeal in seeking after that universal holiness of soul, body and spirit, 'without which no man will see the Lord.'

Indeed this complete new creature is mere madness to a mad world. But it is, notwithstanding, the will and wisdom of God. May we all seek after it!

But some who maintain this doctrine in its full extent are too often guilty of limiting the Almighty. He dispenses his gifts just as he pleases; therefore, it is neither wise nor modest to affirm that a person must be a believer for any length of time before he is capable of receiving a high degree of the Spirit of holiness.

God's usual method is one thing, but his sovereign pleasure is another. He has wise reasons both for hastening and retarding his work. Sometimes he comes suddenly, and unexpected; sometimes not till we have long looked for him.

Indeed it has been my opinion for many years, that one great cause why men make so little improvement in the divine life is their own coldness, negligence and unbelief. And yet I here speak of believers.

May the Spirit of Christ give us a right judgment in all things, and 'fill us with all the fullness of God' (see Eph. 3:19); that so we may be 'mature and complete, not lacking anything' ['perfect and entire, wanting nothing'] (Jas. 1:4 [AV]).

22 February 28th, 1762, is the predicted date for the end of the world

About this same time, five or six honest enthusiasts predicted that the world would end on February 28th. I immediately opposed them, in every possible way, both in public and private. I preached explicitly on the subject, both at West Street and Spitalfields. I warned the society again and again, and spoke to as many individuals as I could; and I saw the fruit of my labour. These enthusiasts made very few converts, hardly thirty in our whole society, I believe. Nevertheless, they made a huge noise, gave a great opportunity to those who were always on the lookout to oppose me and so greatly increased both the number and courage of those who opposed Christian Perfection.

Some questions, now published by one of these
enthusiasts, induced a plain man to write the following:

> QUERIES, humbly proposed to those who deny
> perfection to be attainable in this life.
>
> 1   Has there not been a larger measure of the Holy
> Spirit given under the gospel, than under the Jewish
> dispensation? If not, in what sense was the Spirit not
> given before Christ was glorified (John 7:39)?
>
> 2   Were the 'glories that would follow the suffer-
> ings of Christ' (see 1 Pet. 1:11) an external glory, or an
> internal, i.e., the glory of holiness?
>
> 3   Has God anywhere in scripture commanded us
> more than he has promised to us?
>
> 4   Are the promises of God respecting holiness to
> be fulfilled in this life, or only in the next?
>
> 5   Is a Christian under any other laws than those
> which God promises to 'write on our hearts' (Jer.
> 31:31–3; Heb. 8:10).
>
> 6   In what sense are 'the righteous requirements of
> the law fully met in us, who do not live according to the
> sinful nature but according to the Spirit' (see Rom.
> 8:4)?
>
> 7   Is it impossible for any one in this life to 'love
> God with all his heart, and mind, and soul, and
> strength' (see Matt. 22:37)? And is the Christian under
> any law which is not fulfilled in this love?
>
> 8   Does the soul's going out of the body effect its
> purification from indwelling sin?
>
> 9   If so, is it not something else, not 'the blood of
> Jesus' that 'purifies us from all sin' (1 John. 1:7)?
>
> 10   If his blood purifies us from all sin, while the
> soul and body are united, is it not in this life?
>
> 11   If when the union ceases, is it not in the next?
> And is not this too late?

12   If in the moment of death; what situation is the soul in, when it is neither in the body nor out of it?

13   Has Christ anywhere taught us to pray for what he never designs to give?

14   Has he not taught us to pray, 'your will be done on earth as it is in heaven' (Matt. 6:10)? And is it not done perfectly in heaven?

15   If so, has he not taught us to pray for perfection on earth? Does he not then design to give it?

16   Did not St Paul pray according to the will of God, when he prayed that the Thessalonians might be 'sanctified through and through' (in this world, not the next, unless he was praying for the dead) and their 'whole spirits, souls and bodies be kept blameless at the coming of our Lord Jesus Christ' (see 1 Thess. 5:23)?

17   Do you sincerely desire to be freed from indwelling sin in this life?

18   If you do, did not God give you that desire?

19   If so, did he not give it you to mock you, since it is impossible it should ever be fulfilled?

20   If you have not sincerity enough even to desire it, are you not disputing about matters too high for you?

21   Do you ever pray God to 'cleanse the thoughts of your heart, that you may perfectly love him' (see The Book of Common Prayer, Lord's Supper or Holy Communion, the Collect)?

22   If you neither desire what you ask, nor believe it attainable, are you not praying like a fool?

God help you to consider these questions calmly and impartially!

24   Jane Cooper's letter

Towards the end of this year, God called to himself that burning and shining light, Jane Cooper. As she was both a living and a dying witness of Christian Perfection, it will not be at all foreign to the subject to add a short account of her death; from one of her own letters, containing a plain and ingenuous account of the way in which it pleased God to work that great change in her soul:

May 2nd, 1761

I believe while memory remains in me, gratitude will continue. From the time you preached on Galatians, chapter 5, verse 5 ('But by faith we eagerly await through the Spirit the righteousness for which we hope'), I saw clearly the true state of my soul. That sermon described my heart, and what it wanted to be; namely, truly happy. You read Mr M.'s letter, and it described the religion which I desired. From that time the prize appeared in view, and I was enabled to follow hard after it. I was kept watching unto prayer, sometimes in much distress, at other times in patient expectation of the blessing. For some days before you left London, my soul was stayed on a promise I had applied to me in prayer: 'Then suddenly the Lord you are seeking will come to his temple' (Mal. 3:1). I believed he would, and that he would sit there as a refiner's fire.

The Tuesday after you went, I thought I could not sleep unless he fulfilled his word that night. I never knew as I did then the force of these words: 'Be still, and know that I am God' (Ps. 46:10). I became nothing before him, and enjoyed perfect calmness in my soul. I knew not whether he had destroyed my sin; but I desired to know, that I might praise him. Yet I soon found the return of unbelief, and groaned, being burdened.

On Wednesday I went to London, and sought the Lord without ceasing. I promised, if he would save me from sin, I would praise him. I could part with all things, so I might win Christ. But I found all these pleas to be nothing worth; and that if he saved me, it must be freely, for his own name's sake.

On Thursday I was so much tempted, that I thought of destroying myself, or never conversing more with the people of God: and yet I had no doubt of his pardoning love; but,

> 'Twas worse than death my God to love,
> And not my God alone.

On Friday my distress was deepened. I endeavoured to pray, and could not. I went to Mrs D., who prayed for me, and told me it was the death of nature. I opened the Bible, on 'the cowardly, the unbelieving . . . their place will be in the fiery lake of burning sulphur' (Rev. 21:8). I could not bear it. I opened it again, at Mark, chapter 16, verses 6–7: '"Don't be alarmed . . . You are looking for Jesus the Nazarene . . . go, tell his disciples . . . 'He is going ahead of you into Galilee. There you will see him.'"' I was encouraged, and enabled to pray, believing I should see Jesus at home. I returned that night, and found Mrs G. She prayed for me; and the Predestinarian had no plea, but, 'Lord, you are no respecter of people.' He proved he was not, by blessing me. I was in a moment enabled to lay hold of Jesus Christ, and found salvation by simple faith. He assured me, the Lord, the King, was in the midst of me, and that I should see evil no more. I now blessed him who had visited and redeemed me, and was become my 'wisdom . . . righteousness, holiness and redemption' (see 1 Cor. 1:30). I saw Jesus altogether lovely, and knew he was mine in all his beneficial work. And, glory be to him, he now reigns in my heart without a rival. I find no will but his. I feel no pride; nor any affection but what is placed on him. I know it is by faith I stand; and that watching unto prayer must be the guard of faith. I am happy in God this moment, and I believe for the next. I have often read the chapter you mention (1 Cor. 13), and compared my heart and life with it. In so doing, I feel my shortcomings, and the need I have of the atoning blood. Yet I dare not say, I do not feel a measure of the love there described, though I am not all I shall be. I desire to be lost in that 'love which passeth knowledge' (see 1 Cor. 13:8). I see 'the righteous will live by his faith' (Hab. 2:4), and to me, who is 'the least of all God's people' (Eph. 3:8), this grace is given. If I were an archangel, I should veil my face before him, and let silence speak his praise!

The following account is given by one who saw and heard what she relates:

1 In the beginning of November, she seemed to have a foresight of what was coming on her, and used frequently to sing these words:

> When pain o'er this weak flesh prevails,
> With lamb-like patience arm my breast.

And when she sent to me, to let me know she was ill, she wrote in her note, 'I suffer the will of Jesus. All he sends is sweetened by his love. I am as happy as if I heard a voice say,

> "For me my elder brethren stay,
> And angels beckon me away,
> And Jesus bids me come!"'

2 Upon my telling her, 'I cannot choose life or death for you,' she said, 'I asked the Lord, that, if it was his will, I might die first. And he told me, you should survive me, and that you should close my eyes.'

When we perceived it was the smallpox, I said to her, 'My dear, you will not be frightened if we tell you what is your illness.'

She said, 'I cannot be frightened at God's will.'

3   The distemper was soon very heavy on her; but so much the more was her faith strengthened. Tuesday, November 16th, she said to me, 'I have been worshipping before the throne in a glorious manner; my soul was so let into God!'

I said, 'Did the Lord give you any particular promise?'

'No,' she replied, 'it was all —

"That sacred awe that dares not move,
And all the silent heaven of love."'

4   On Thursday, I asked, 'What have you to say to me?'

She replied, 'Nothing except what you know already; God is love.'

I asked, 'Have you any particular promise?'

She replied, 'I do not seem to want any; I can live without. I shall die a lump of deformity, but shall meet you all glorious. And, meantime, I shall still have fellowship with your spirit.'

5   Mr M. asked what she thought the most excellent way to walk in, and what were its chief hindrances. She answered: 'The greatest hindrance is generally from the natural constitution. It was mine to be reserved, to be very quiet, to suffer much and to say little. Some may think one way more excellent, and some another. But the thing is to live in the will of God. For some months past, when I have been particularly devoted to this, I have felt such a guidance of his Spirit, and the anointing which I have received from the Holy One has so taught me about all things, that I did not need any man to teach me, except as this anointing teaches.'

6   On Friday morning she said, 'I believe I shall die.' She then sat up in her bed and said, 'Lord, I bless you, that you are always with me, and all you have is mine. Your love is greater than my weakness, greater than my helplessness, greater than my unworthiness. Lord,

you say *to corruption, You are my sister!* And glory be to you, O Jesus, you are my Brother. Let me together with all the saints, grasp how wide and long and high and deep is the love of Christ (see Eph. 3:18). Bless these' (some that were present), 'let them be every moment exercised in all things as you would have them to be.'

7　Some hours after, it seemed as if the agonies of death were just coming upon her, but her face was full of smiles of triumph, and she clapped her hands for joy. Mrs C. said, 'My dear, you are more than conqueror through the blood of the Lamb.'

She answered: 'Yes, O yes, sweet Jesus! O death, where is your sting?' She then lay as in a doze for some time. Afterwards, she tried to speak, but could not. However, she testified her love by shaking hands with all in the room.

8　Mr W. then came. She said, 'Sir, I did not know that I should live to see you. But I am glad the Lord has given me this opportunity, and likewise power to speak to you. I love you. You have always preached the strictest doctrine, and I loved to follow it. Do so still, whoever is pleased or displeased.'

He asked, 'Do you now believe you are saved from sin?'

She said, 'Yes, I have had no doubt of it for many months. That I ever had was because I did not abide in the faith. I now feel I have kept the faith; and perfect love drives out all fear. As to you, the Lord promised me, your latter works should exceed your former, though I do not live to see it. I have been a great enthusiast, as they term it, these six months; but never lived so near the heart of Christ in my life. You, sir, desire to comfort the hearts of hundreds by following that simplicity your soul loves.'

9　To one who had received the love of God under her prayer, she said, 'I feel I have not followed "cleverly invented stories" (2 Pet. 1:16), for I am as happy as

I can live. Do you press on, and stop not short of the mark.'

To Miss M. she said, 'Love Christ, he loves you. I believe I shall see you at the right hand of God. But, "star differs from star in splendour. So will it be with the resurrection" (1 Cor. 15:41–2). I charge you, in the presence of God, meet me on that day all glorious within. Avoid all conformity to the world. You are robbed of many of your privileges. I know I shall be found blameless. Labour to be found "blameless and at peace with him" (2 Pet. 3:14).'

10   On Saturday morning, she prayed nearly as follows: 'I know, my Lord, my life is prolonged only to do your will. And though I should never eat or drink more' (she had not swallowed anything for nearly twenty-eight hours), 'your will be done. I am willing to be kept so for twelve months. "Man does not live on bread alone" (Matt. 4:4). I praise you that there is not a shadow of complaining in our streets. In that sense we know not what sickness means. Indeed, Lord, "neither death nor life, neither the present nor the future, nor anything else in all creation, will be able to separate us from the love of God" (see Rom. 8:38–9) for one moment. Bless these, that there may be no lack in their souls. I believe there shall not. I pray in faith.'

On Sunday and Monday she was light-headed, but sensible at times. It then plainly appeared, her heart was still in heaven. Someone said to her, 'Jesus is our mark.'

She replied, 'I have but one mark, I am all spiritual.'

Miss M. said to her, 'You dwell in God.'

She answered: 'Altogether.'

A person asked her: 'Do you love me?'

She said, 'O, I love Christ, I love my Christ.'

To another she said, 'I shall not long be here, Jesus is precious, very precious indeed.'

She said to Miss M., 'The Lord is very good, he keeps my soul above all.'

For fifteen hours before she died, she had severe convulsions. Her suffering was extreme. Someone said, 'You are made perfect through sufferings.'

She said, 'More and more so.' After lying quiet some time, she said, 'Lord, you are strong!' Then pausing a considerable space, she uttered her last words, 'My Jesus is all in all to me. Glory be to him through time and eternity.' After this, she lay still for about half an hour, and then expired without a sigh or groan.

25   *Further Thoughts on Christian Perfection*

The next year, the number of those who believed they were saved from sin further increased and I thought it necessary to publish, especially for them to use, Further Thoughts on Christian Perfection.

QUESTION 1   How is 'Christ the end of the law so that there may be righteousness for everyone who believes' (see Rom. 10:4)?

ANSWER   In order to understand this, you must understand what law is here spoken of, and this, I apprehend, is,

1   The Mosaic law, the whole Mosaic dispensation; which St Paul continually speaks of as one, though containing three parts, the political, moral, and ceremonial.

2   The Adamic law, that given to Adam in innocence, properly called 'the law of works'. This is in substance the same with the angelic law, being common to angels and men. It required that man should use, to the glory of God, all the powers with which he was created. Now, he was created free from any defect, either in his understanding or his affections. His body did not impede his mind; it did not hinder his apprehending all things clearly, judging truly concerning them, and reasoning

justly, if he reasoned at all. I say, *if he reasoned*, for possibly he did not. Perhaps he had no need of reasoning, till his corruptible body pressed down the mind, and impaired its native faculties. Perhaps, till then, the mind saw every truth that offered as directly as the eye now sees the light.

Consequently, this law, fashioned to his original powers, required that he should always think, always speak, and always act precisely right, in every point whatever. He was well able so to do. And God could not but require the service he was able to pay.

But Adam fell, and his incorruptible body became corruptible; and ever since it impedes the soul and hinders its operations. Hence, at present, no child of man can at all times apprehend clearly, or judge truly. And where either the judgment or apprehension is wrong, it is impossible to reason justly. Therefore, it is as natural for a man to mistake as to breathe; and he can no more live without the one than without the other. Consequently, no man is able to perform the service which the Adamic law requires.

And no man is obliged to perform it; God does not require it of any man. For Christ is the end of the Adamic, as well as the Mosaic, law. By his death, he has put an end to both, he has abolished both the one and the other with regard to man; and the obligation to observe either the one or the other is vanished away. Nor is any man living bound to observe the Adamic more than the Mosaic law. [John Wesley's own footnote adds: I mean, it is not the condition either of present or future salvation.]

In this connection, Christ has established another law, namely, the law of faith. Not every one who does, but every one who believes now receives righteousness, in the full sense of the word, that is, he is justified, sanctified and glorified.

Q 2 Are we then dead to the law?

A We are 'dead to the law through the body of Christ' (see Rom. 7:4), to the Adamic as well as Mosaic law. We are wholly freed therefrom by his death; that law expiring with him.

Q 3 How, then, are we 'not free from God's law but under Christ's law' (see 1 Cor. 9:21)?

A We are without that law, but it does not follow that we are without any law. For God has established another law in its place, even the law of faith. And we are all under this law to God and to Christ; both our Creator and our Redeemer require us to observe it.

Q 4 Is love the fulfilling of this law?

A Unquestionably it is. The whole law under which we now are, is fulfilled by love (Rom. 13:9–10). Faith working or animated by love is all that God now requires of man. He has substituted (not sincerity, but) love, in the room of angelic perfection.

Q 5 How is 'the goal of this command is love' (1 Tim. 1:5)?

A It is the goal of every commandment of God. It is the point aimed at by the whole and every part of the Christian institution. The foundation is faith, purifying the heart; the goal is love, persevering a good conscience.

Q 6 What love is this?

A The loving the Lord our God with all our heart, mind, soul, and strength; and the loving our neighbour, every man, as ourselves, as our own souls.

Q 7 What are the fruits or properties of this love?

A St Paul informs us at large, love is patient. It suffers all the weaknesses of the children of God, all the wickedness of the children of the world; and that not for a little time only, but as long as God pleases. In all, it sees the hand of God, and willingly submits thereto. Meantime, it is kind. In all, and after all, it suffers, it is soft, mild, tender, benign. 'Love does not envy', it excludes every kind and degree of envy out of the heart. 'Love does not act rashly' in a violent, headstrong manner, nor pass any rash or severe judgment. 'Love does not behave itself indecently', it is not rude, does not act out of character. 'Love is not self-seeking' for her own ease, pleasure, honour, or profit. 'Love is not easily angered', love expels all anger from the heart. Love keeps no record of wrongs, and casts out all jealousy, suspiciousness, and readiness to believe evil. 'Love does not delight in evil', but weeps at the sin or folly of its bitterest enemies. 'Love rejoices in the truth'; in the holiness and happiness of every child of man. 'Love covers all things' and speaks evil about nobody. 'Love believes all things' that are to the advantage of another's character. 'Love hopes all things' whatever may extenuate the faults which cannot be denied; and love 'endures all things' which God can permit, or men and devils inflict (1 Cor. 13:4–7). This is 'the law of Christ, the perfect law, the law of freedom.'

And this distinction between the 'law of faith' (or love) and 'the law of works', is neither a subtle nor an unnecessary distinction. It is plain, easy and intelligible to any common understanding. And it is absolutely necessary, to prevent a thousand doubts and fears, even in those who do 'walk in love.'

Q 8 'If we stumble at just one point of the law are we not guilty of breaking it all' (see Jas. 2:10)? Yes, the best of us, even against this law?

A In one sense we do not, while all our attitudes, and thoughts, and words, and works spring from love. But in another we do, and shall do, more or less, as long as we remain in the body. For neither love nor the 'anointing of the Holy One' makes us infallible. Therefore, through unavoidable defect of understanding, we cannot but mistake in many things. And these mistakes will frequently give rise to something wrong in our frames of mind, and words and actions. From mistaking his character, we may love a person less than he really deserves. And by the same mistake we are unavoidably led to speak or act, with regard to that person, in such a manner as is contrary to this law, in some or other of the preceding instances.

Q 9 Do we not then need Christ, even on this account?

A The holiest of men still need Christ, as their Prophet, as 'the light of the world' (John 8:12). For he does not give them light, but from moment to moment. The instant he withdraws, all is darkness. They still need Christ as their king, for God does not give them a stock of holiness. But unless they receive a supply every moment, nothing but unholiness would remain. They still need Christ as their priest, to make atonement for their holy things. Even perfect holiness is acceptable to God only through Jesus Christ.

Q 10 May not, then, the very best of men adopt the dying martyr's confession: 'I am in myself nothing but sin, darkness, hell; but you are my light, my holiness, my heaven'?

A Not exactly. But the best of men may say, 'You are my light, my holiness, my heaven. Through my union with you, I am full of light, of holiness, and happiness. But if I were left to myself, I should be nothing but sin, darkness, hell.'

But to proceed: The best of men need Christ as their priest, their atonement, their advocate with the Father, not only as the continuance of their every blessing depends on his death and intercession, but on account of their coming short of the law of love. For every man living does so. You who feel all love, compare yourselves with the preceding description. Weigh yourselves in the balance, and see if you are not wanting in many particulars.

Q 11 But if all this be consistent with Christian Perfection, that perfection is not freedom from all sin; since 'sin is the breaking of the law'; and the perfect break the very law they are under. Besides, they need atonement of Christ; and he is the atonement of nothing but sin. Is, then, the term, *sinless perfection*, proper?

A It is not worth arguing about. But observe in what

sense the persons in question need the atonement of Christ. They do not need him to reconcile them to God afresh, for they are reconciled. They do not need him to restore the favour of God, but to continue it. He does not procure pardon for them anew, but he 'always lives to intercede for them' (Heb. 7:25), and 'by one sacrifice he has made perfect for ever those who are being made holy' (Heb. 10:14).

For want of duly considering this, some deny that they need the atonement of Christ. Indeed, exceeding few, I do not remember to have found five of them in England. Of the two, I would sooner give up perfection, but we need not give up either one or the other. The perfection I hold, love 'being joyful always, praying continually; and giving thanks in all circumstances' (see 1 Thess. 5:16–18), is well consistent with it; if any hold a perfection which is not, they must look to it.

Q 12 Does then Christian Perfection imply any more than sincerity?

A Not if you mean by that word, love filling the heart, expelling pride, anger, desire, self-will; being joyful always, praying continually; and giving thanks in all circumstances. But, I doubt few use sincerity in this sense. Therefore, I think the old word is best.

A person may be sincere who has all his natural dispositions, pride, anger, lust, self-will. But he is not perfect till his heart is cleansed from these, and all its other corruptions.

To clear this point a little further: I know many that love God with all their heart. He is their one desire, their one delight, and they are continually happy in him. They love their neighbour as themselves. They feel as sincere, fervent, constant a desire for happiness of every man, good or bad, friend or enemy, as for their own. They rejoice evermore, pray without ceasing, and in everything give thanks. Their souls are continually streaming up to God, in holy joy, prayer, and praise. This is a point of fact; and this is plain, sound, scriptural experience.

But even these souls dwell in a shattered body, and are so pressed down thereby, that they cannot always exert themselves as they would, by thinking, speaking, and acting precisely right. For lack of better bodily organs, they must at times think, speak, or act wrong; not indeed through a defect of love, but through a defect of knowledge. And while this is the case, notwithstanding that defect and its consequences, they fulfil the law of love.

Yet as, even in this case, there is not a full conformity to the perfect law, so the most perfect do, on this very account, need the blood of atonement, and may properly for themselves, as well as for their brethren, say, 'Forgive us our sins.'

Q 13 But if Christ has put an end to that law, what is the need of any atonement for their transgressing it?

A Observe in what sense he has put an end to it, and the difficulty vanishes. Were it not for the abiding merit of his death, and his continual intercession for us, the law would condemn us still. These, therefore, we still need for every transgression of it.

Q 14 But can one that is saved from sin be tempted?

A Yes, for Christ was tempted.

Q 15 However, what you call temptation, I call the corruption of my heart. And how will you distinguish one from the other?

A In some cases it is impossible to distinguish, without the direct witness of the Spirit. But in general one may distinguish thus:

One commends me. Here is a temptation to pride. But instantly my soul is humbled before God. And I feel no pride, of which I am as sure, as that pride is not humility.

A man strikes me. Here is a temptation to anger. But my heart overflows with love. And I feel no anger at all, of which I can be as sure as that love and anger are not the same.

A woman solicits me. Here is a temptation to lust. But

in the instant I shrink back. And I feel no desire or lust at all, of which I can be as sure as that my hand is cold or hot.

Thus it is, if I am tempted by a present object; and it is just the same, if, when it is absent, the devil recalls a commendation, an injury, or a woman, to my mind. In the instant the soul repels the temptation, and remains filled with pure love.

And the difference is still plainer, when I compare my present state with my past, wherein I felt temptation and corruption, too.

Q 16 But how do you know, that you are sanctified, saved from your inbred corruption?

A I can know it no otherwise than I know that I am justified. 'And this is how we know that he lives in us': in either sense, 'We know it by the Spirit he gave us' (1 John 3:24).

We know it by the witness and by the fruit of the Spirit. And, first, by the witness. As, when we were justified, the Spirit bore witness with our spirit, that our sins were forgiven; so, when we were sanctified, he bore witness that they are taken away. Indeed, the witness of sanctification is not always clear at first (as neither is that of justification); neither is it afterwards the same, but, like that of justification, sometimes stronger and sometimes fainter. Yes, and sometimes it is withdrawn. Yet, in general, the latter testimony of the Spirit is both as clear and as steady as the former.

Q 17 But what need is there of it, seeing sanctification is a real change, not a relative change only, like justification?

A But is the new birth a relative change only? Is not this a real change? Therefore, if we need no witness of our sanctification, because it is a real change, for the same reason we should need none, that we are born of or are the children of God.

Q 18 But does not sanctification shine by its own light?

A   And does not the new birth, too? Sometimes it does, and so does sanctification, at others it does not. In the hour of temptation Satan clouds the work of God, and injects various doubts and reasonings, especially in those who have either very weak or very strong understandings. At such times there is absolute need of that witness; without which the work of sanctification not only could not be discerned, but could no longer exist. Were it not for this, the soul could not then abide in the love of God, much less could it be joyful always and give thanks in all circumstances. In these situations, therefore, a direct testimony that we are sanctified is necessary in the highest degree.

'But I have no witness that I am saved from sin. And yet I have no doubt of it.' Very well; as long as you have no doubt, it is enough; when you have, you will need that witness.

Q   19   But what scripture makes mention of any such thing, or gives any reason to expect it?

A   That scripture, 'We have not received the spirit of the world but the Spirit who is from God, that we may understand what God has freely given us' (1 Cor. 2:12).

Now surely sanctification is one of the things 'freely given us by God'. And no possible reason can be assigned why this should be excepted, when the apostle says, 'we receive the Spirit', for this very end, 'that we may understand what God' thus 'has freely given us'.

Is not the same thing implied in that well-known scripture, 'The Spirit himself testifies with our spirit that we are God's children' (Rom. 8:16). Does he witness this only to those who are children of God in the lowest sense? No, but to those also who are such in the highest sense. And does he not witness, that they are such in the highest sense? What reason have we to doubt it?

What, if a man were to affirm (as indeed many do) that this witness belongs only to the highest class of Christians? Would not you answer, 'The apostle makes no restriction; therefore doubtless it belongs to all the children of God?' And will not the same answer hold, if any affirm, that it belongs only to the lowest class?

Consider likewise 1 John, chapter 5, verse 19: 'We know that we are children of God.' How? 'And this is how we know that he lives in us: We know it by the Spirit he gave us' (1 John 3:24). And what ground have we, either from scripture or reason, to exclude the witness, any more than the fruit of the Spirit from being here intended? By this then also 'we know that we are children of God', and in what sense we are so; whether we are babies, young men, or fathers, we know in the same manner.

Not that I affirm that all young men, or even fathers, have this testimony every moment. There may be intervals between the direct testimony that they are thus born of God; but those intervals are fewer and shorter as they grow up in Christ, and some have the testimony both of their justification and sanctification, without any interval at all; which I presume more might have, had they walked humbly and closely with God.

Q 20 May not some of them have a testimony from the Spirit, that they shall not finally fall from God?

A They may. And this persuasion, that neither life nor death shall separate them from him, far from being hurtful, may in some circumstances be extremely useful. These therefore we should in no way grieve, but earnestly encourage them to 'hold firmly till the end the confidence we had at first' (Heb. 3:14).

Q 21 But have any a testimony from the Spirit that they shall never sin?

A We know not what God may vouchsafe to some particular persons; but we do not find any general state described in scripture, from which a man cannot draw back to sin. If there were any state wherein this was impossible, it would be that of these who are sanctified, who are 'fathers in Christ, always joyful, praying continually, and giving thanks in all circumstances'; but it is not impossible for those to draw back. They who are sanctified, yet may fall and perish (see Heb. 10:29). Even fathers in Christ need that warning: 'Do not love the world' (1 John 2:15). They who 'are joyful, pray', and 'give thanks in all circumstances', may, nevertheless 'put out the Spirit's fire' (1 Thess. 5:19). And even they who are 'sealed for the day of redemption', may yet 'grieve the Holy Spirit of God' (Eph. 4:30).

Although, therefore, God may give such a witness to some particular persons, yet it is not to be expected by Christians in general; there being no scripture whereon to ground such an expectation.

Q 22 By what 'fruit of the Spirit' may we 'know that we are of God, even in the highest sense'?

A By love, joy, peace, always abiding; by invariable patience, giving oneself over to God; by gentleness, triumphing over all provocation; by goodness, mildness, sweetness, tenderness of spirit; by faithfulness, simplicity, godly sincerity; by meekness, calmness, evenness of spirit; by temperance, not only in food and sleep, but in all things natural and spiritual.

Q 23 But what great matter is there in this? Have we not all this when we are justified?

A What, total giving oneself over to the will of God, without the least love of the creature, but in and for God, excluding all pride? Love to man, excluding all envy, all jealousy and rash judging? Meekness, keeping the whole soul in unbroken calm, and temperance in all things? Deny that any ever came up to this, if you please; but do not say, all who are justified do.

Q 24 But some who are newly justified do. What then will you say to these?

A If they really do, I will say they are sanctified; saved from sin in that moment; and that they never need lose what God has given, or feel sin any more.

But certainly this is an exceptional case. It is otherwise

with the majority of those who are justified. They feel in themselves more or less pride, anger, self-will, a heart bent to backsliding. And, till they have gradually mortified these, they are not fully renewed in love.

Q 25 But is not this the case with all who are justified? Do they not gradually die to sin and grow in grace, till at, or perhaps a little before, death God perfects them in love?

A I believe this is the case of most, but not all. God usually gives a considerable time for men to receive light, to grow in grace, to do and suffer his will, before they are either justified or sanctified, but he does not invariably adhere to this; sometimes he 'cuts short his work'. He does the work of many years in a few weeks; perhaps in a week, a day, an hour. He justifies or sanctifies both those who have done or suffered nothing, and who have not had time for a gradual growth either in light or grace. And 'does he not have the right to do what he wants with his own money? Or are you envious because he is generous?' (see Matt. 20:15).

It need not, therefore, be affirmed over and over and proved by forty texts of scripture, either that most men are perfected in love at last, that there is a gradual work of God in the soul, or that, generally speaking, it is a long time, even many years, before sin is destroyed. All this we know. But we know likewise, that God may, with man's co-operation, 'cut short his work', in whatever stage he pleases, and do the usual work of many years in a moment. He does so in many instances, and yet there is a gradual work, both before and after that moment; so that one may affirm the work is gradual, another, it is instantaneous, without any kind of contradiction.

Q 26 Does St Paul mean any more by being 'marked . . . with a seal, the promised Holy Spirit' (Eph. 1:13), than being 'renewed in love'?

A Perhaps in one place (see 2 Cor. 1:22) he does not mean so much, but in another (see Eph. 1:13) he seems to include both the fruit and the witness; and that in a higher degree than we experience even when we are first 'renewed in love'. 'You were marked in him with a seal, the promised Holy Spirit' (Eph. 1:13), when God made 'our hope sure' (see Heb. 6:11). Such a confidence of receiving all the promises of God, excluding the possibility of doubting; with that Holy Spirit, by universal holiness, stamping the whole image of God on our hearts.

Q 27   But how can those who are thus sealed, 'grieve the Holy Spirit of God' (Eph. 4:30)?

A   St Paul tells you very particularly,

1   By such conversation which is not profitable, which does not edify, and is not apt to minister grace to the hearer.

2   By relapsing into bitterness or lack of kindness.

3   By wrath, lasting displeasure, or lack of tender-heartedness.

4   By anger, however soon it is over; lack of instantly forgiving one another.

5   By clamour or bawling, loud, harsh, rough speaking.

6   By evil-speaking, whispering, tale-bearing, needlessly mentioning the fault of an absent person, though in ever so soft a manner.

Q 28   What do you think of those in London, who seem to have been lately 'renewed in love'?

A   There is something very unusual in the experience of the greater part of them. One would expect that a believer should first be filled with love, and so be emptied of sin; whereas these were emptied of sin first, and then filled with love. Perhaps it pleased God to work in this manner, to make his work more plain and undeniable, and to distinguish it more clearly from that overflowing love, which is often felt even in a justified state.

It seems likewise most agreeable to the great promise, 'I will cleanse you from all your impurities and from all your idols. I will give you a new heart and put a new spirit in you' (Ezek. 36:25–6).

But I do not think of them all alike. There is a wide difference between some of them and others. I think most of them with whom I have spoken, have much faith, love, joy and peace. Some of these I believe are renewed in love, and have the direct witness of it; and they manifest the fruit above described in all their words and actions. Now, let any man call this what he will, it is what I call perfection.

But some who have much love, peace, and joy, yet have not the direct witness; and others who think they have, are, nevertheless, displaying a lack in the fruit. How many I will not say, perhaps one in ten, perhaps fewer. But some are undeniably lacking in patience and Christian resignation. They do not see the hand of God in whatever occurs, and cheerfully embrace it. They do not give thanks in all circumstances and they are not joyful always. They are not happy, at least, not always happy, for sometimes they complain. They say, this or that is hard!

Some are lacking in gentleness. They resist evil, instead of turning the other cheek. They do not receive reproach with gentleness, no, nor even reproof. No, they are not able to bear contradiction, without the appearance, at least, of resentment. If they are reproved or contradicted, though mildly, they do not take it well, they behave with more distance and reserve than they did before. If they are reproved or contradicted harshly, they answer it with harshness, with a loud voice, or with an angry tone, or in a sharp and surly manner. They speak sharply or roughly when they reprove others, and behave roughly to their inferiors.

Some are lacking in goodness. They are not kind, mild, sweet, amiable, soft, and loving at all times, in their spirit, in their words, in their look and air, in the whole tenor of their behaviour; and that to all, high and low, rich and poor, without respect of persons; particularly to them that are out of the way, to opposers, and to those of their own household. They do not long, study, endeavour, by every means, to make all about them happy. They can see them uneasy, and not be concerned; perhaps they make them so; and then wipe their mouths and say, 'Why, they deserve it, it is their own fault.'

Some are lacking in faithfulness, a nice regard to truth, simplicity, and godly sincerity. Their love is hardly without pretence; something like guile is found in their mouth. To avoid being rough, they lean to the other extreme. They are so excessively smooth that they scarcely avoid a degree of fawning, or of seeming to mean what they do not.

Some are lacking in meekness, quietness of spirit, composure, evenness of temper. They are up and down, sometimes high, sometimes low. Their mind is not well balanced. Their affections are either not in the due proportion – they have too much of one, too little of another – or they are not duly mixed and tempered together, so as to balance each other. Hence there is often a jar. Their soul is out of tune, and cannot make the true harmony.

Some are lacking in self-control. They do not steadily use that kind and amount of food which they know, or might know, would be most conducive to the health, strength, and vigour of the body. Or they are not self-controlled in sleep, they do not rigorously adhere to what is best both for body and mind, otherwise they would constantly go to bed and rise early, and at a fixed hour. Or they eat late, which is neither good for body nor soul. Or they use neither fasting nor abstinence. Or they prefer (which are in so many ways lacking in self-control) that preaching, reading, or conversation, which gives them transient joy and comfort, before that which brings godly sorrow, or instruction in righteousness. Such joy is not sanctified, it does not tend to, and terminate in, the crucifixion of the heart. Such faith does not centre in God, but rather in itself.

So far all is plain. I believe you have faith, and love, and joy, and peace. Yet you who are particularly concerned know each for yourself, that you are lacking in the above-mentioned respects. You are lacking either in patience, gentleness, or goodness; or in faithfulness, gentleness or self-control. Let us not, then, on either hand, fight about words. In this matter we clearly agree.

You have not what I call perfection, if others will call it so, they may. However, hold fast what you have, and earnestly pray for what you have not.

Q   29   Can those who are perfect grow in grace?

A   Undoubtedly they can, and that not only while they are in the body, but to all eternity.

Q   30   Can they fall from it?

A   I am well assured they can; the facts put this beyond dispute. Formerly we thought one saved from sin could not fall, now we know the opposite. We are surrounded with instances of those who recently experienced all that I mean by perfection. They had both the fruit of the Spirit and the witness, but they have now lost both. Neither does any one stand by virtue of anything that is implied in the nature of the state. There is no such height or strength of holiness as it is impossible to fall from. If there be any that cannot fall, this wholly depends on the promise of God.

Q   31   Can those who fall from this state regain it?

A   Why not? We have many instances of this also. In fact, it is an exceeding common thing for people to lose it more than once, before they are established in it.

It is therefore to guard those who are saved from sin, from every occasion of stumbling, that I give the following advices. But first I shall speak plainly concerning the work itself.

I esteem this late work to be of God, probably the greatest now on earth. Yet, like all others, this also is mixed with much human frailty. But these weaknesses are far less than might have been expected, and ought to have been joyfully borne by all that loved and followed after righteousness. That there have been a few weak, hot-headed men, is no reproach to the work itself, no just ground for accusing a multitude of thoughtful men who are patterns of strict holiness. Yet (just the contrary to what ought to have been) the opposition is great; the helps few. Hereby many are hindered from seeking faith and holiness by the false zeal of others, and some who at first began to run well are turned out of the way.

Q 32   What is the first advice [These advices which follow were published in a separate tract in 1762, under the title, *Cautions and Directions given to the Greatest Professors in the Methodist Societies*] that you would give them?

A   Watch and pray continually against pride. If God has cast it out, see that it enter no more. It is just as dangerous as desire. And you may slide back into it unawares, especially if you think there is no danger of it. 'No, but I ascribe all I have to God.' So you may, and be proud nevertheless. For it is pride not only to ascribe anything we have to ourselves, but to think we have what we really have not. Mr L., for instance, ascribed all the light he had to God, and so he was humble, but then he thought he had more light than any man living, and this was evident pride. So you ascribe all the knowledge you have to God, and in this respect you are humble. But if you think you have more than you really have, or if you think you are so taught of God, as no longer to need man's teaching, pride lies at the door. Yes, you have need to be taught, not only by Mr Morgan, by one another, by Mr Maxfield, or me, but by the weakest preacher in London, yes, by all men. For God sendeth by whom he will send.

Do not therefore say to any who would advise or reprove you, 'You are blind, you cannot teach me.' Do not say, 'This is your wisdom, your human reason', but calmly weigh the thing before God.

Always remember, much grace does not imply much

light. These do not always go together. As there may be much light where there is little love, so there may be much love where there is little light. The heart has more heat than the eye, yet it cannot see. And God has wisely tempered the members of the body together, that none of them may say to another, 'I don't need you' (1 Cor. 12:21)!

To imagine none can teach you, but those who are themselves saved from sin, is a very great and dangerous mistake. Give not place to it for a moment. It would lead you into a thousand other mistakes, and that irrecoverably. No, dominion is not founded on grace, as the madmen of the last age talked. Obey and regard 'those who are over you in the Lord' and do not think you know better than they do. Know their place and your own; always remembering, much love does not imply much light.

Not observing this has led some into many mistakes, and into the appearance, at least, of pride. O beware of the appearance, and the thing! 'Your attitude should be the same as that of Christ Jesus' (Phil. 2:5). All of you, 'Clothe yourselves with humility' (1 Pet. 5:5). Let it not only fill, but cover you all over. Let modesty and self-diffidence appear in all your words and actions. Let all you say and do show that you are little, and base, and mean, and vile in your own eyes.

As one instance of this, be always ready to own any fault you have been in. If you have at any time thought, spoken, or acted wrongly, be not backward to acknowledge it. Never dream that this will hurt the cause of God. No, it will further it. Be therefore open and frank, when you are taxed by anything; do not seek either to evade or disguise it. But let it appear just as it is, and you will thereby not hinder, but adorn the gospel.

Q 33 What is the second advice which you give them?

A Beware of that daughter of pride, enthusiasm. O keep at the utmost distance from it! Give no place to a heated imagination. Do not hastily ascribe things to God. Do not easily suppose dreams, voices, impressions, visions, or revelations to be from God. They may be from him. They may be from nature. They may be from the devil. Therefore, 'do not believe every spirit, but test the spirits to see whether they are from God' (1 John 4:1). Try all things by the written word, and let all bow down before it. You are in danger of enthusiasm every hour, if you depart ever so little from scripture, yes, or from the plain, literal meaning of any text, taken in connection with the context. And so you are, if you despise or lightly esteem reason, knowledge, or human learning, every one of which is an excellent gift of God, and may serve the noblest purpose.

I advise you, never to use the words, wisdom, reason, or knowledge, by way of reproach. On the contrary, pray that you yourself may abound in them more and more. If you mean worldly wisdom, useless knowledge, false reasoning, say so; and throw away the chaff, but not the wheat.

One general inlet to enthusiasm is expecting the end without the means, the expecting knowledge, for instance, without searching the scriptures, and consulting the children of God; expecting spiritual strength without constant prayer, and steady watchfulness; expecting any blessing without hearing the word of God at every opportunity.

Some have been ignorant of this device of Satan. They have left off searching the scriptures. They said, 'God writes all the scriptures on my heart. Therefore, I have no need to read it'. Others thought they had not so much need of hearing, and so grew slack in attending the morning preaching. O take warning, you who are concerned herein! You have listened to the voice of a stranger. Flee back to Christ, and keep in the good old way, which was 'once for all entrusted to the saints' (Jude v.3), the way that even a heathen bore testimony of, 'that the Christians rose early every day to sing hymns to Christ as God'.

The very desire of 'growing in grace' may sometimes be an inlet of enthusiasm. As it continually leads us to seek new grace, it may lead us unawares to seek something else new, beside new degrees of love to God and man. So it has led some to seek and fancy they had received gifts of a new kind, after a new heart, as:

1 The loving of God with all our mind;
2 With all our soul;
3 With all our strength;
4 Oneness with God;
5 Oneness with Christ;
6 Having our life hid with Christ in God;
7 Being dead with Christ;
8 Rising with him;
9 The sitting with him in heavenly realm;
10 The being taken up into his throne;
11 The being in the New Jerusalem;
12 The seeing the tabernacle of God come down among men;
13 The being dead to all works;
14 The not being liable to death, pain, or grief, or temptation.

One ground of many of these mistakes is taking every fresh, strong application of any of these scriptures to the heart, to be a gift of a new kind; not knowing that several of these scriptures are not fulfilled yet; that most of the others are fulfilled when we are justified; the rest, the moment we are sanctified. It remains only to experience them in higher degrees. This is all we have to expect.

Another ground of these, and a thousand mistakes, is not considering deeply that love is the highest gift of God; humble, gentle, patient love; that all visions, revelations, manifestations whatever, are little things compared to love; and that all the gifts above-mentioned are either the same with, or infinitely inferior to, it.

It were well you should be thoroughly sensible of this –

the heaven of heavens is love. There is nothing higher in religion; there is, in effect, nothing else; if you look for anything but more love, you are looking wide of the mark, you are getting out of the royal way. And when you are asking others, 'Have you received this or that blessing?' if you mean anything but more love, you mean wrong; you are leading them out of the way, and putting them on a false scent. Settle it then in your heart, that from that moment God has saved you from all sin, you are to aim at nothing more, but more of that love described in 1 Corinthians, chapter 13. You can go no higher than this, till you are carried 'to Abraham's side' (Luke 16:22).

I say yet again, beware of enthusiasm. Such is the imagining you have the gift of prophesying, or the ability to distinguish between spirits, which I do not believe one of you has; no, nor ever had yet. Beware of judging people to be either right or wrong by your own feelings. This is no scriptural way of judging. O keep close to 'the law and to the testimony!'

Q 34 What is the third?

A Beware of antinomianism, 'making void the law', or any part of it, 'through faith'. Enthusiasm naturally leads to this, indeed they can scarce be separated. This may steal on you in a thousand forms, so that you cannot be too watchful against it. Take heed of everything, whether in principle or practice, which has any tendency thereto. Even that great truth, that 'Christ is the end of the law' (Rom. 10:4), may betray us into it, if we do not consider that he has adopted every point of the moral law, and grafted it into the law of love. Beware of thinking, 'Because I am filled with love, I need not have so much holiness. Because I pray always, therefore I need no set time for private prayer. Because I watch always, therefore I need no particular self-examination.' Let us 'make his law', the whole written word, 'great and glorious' (Isa. 42:21). Let this be our voice: 'I prize your commandments above gold or precious stones. O what love I have of your law! All the day long I study it.'

Beware of antinomian books, particularly the works of Dr Crisp and Mr Saltmarsh. They contain many excellent things, and this makes them the more dangerous. O be warned in time! Do not play with fire. Do not put your hand on the hole of the cobra's den (see Isa. 11:8). I entreat you, beware of bigotry. Let not your love or good deeds be confined to Methodists, so called, only; much less to that very small part of them who seem to be renewed in love; or to those who believe your and their reports. O make not this your shibboleth! Beware of still-ness, ceasing in a wrong sense from your own works. To mention one instance of many: 'You have received', says one, 'a great blessing. But you began to talk of it, and to do this and this, so you lost it. You should have been still.'

Beware of self-indulgence, yes, and making a virtue of it, laughing at self-denial, and taking up the cross daily, at fasting or abstinence. Beware of censoriousness, thinking or calling them that in any way oppose you, whether in judgment or practice, blind, dead, fallen, or 'enemies of the work'. Once more, beware of believing that faith alone, apart from works, is sufficient for justification, cry-ing nothing but, 'Believe, believe!' and condemning those as ignorant or legal who speak in a more scriptural way. At certain seasons, indeed, it may be right to think about nothing but repentance, or merely of faith, or altogether of holiness; but, in general, our call is to declare the whole will of God, and to prophesy according to the proportion of faith. The written word treats of the whole and every particular branch of righteousness, descending to its minutest branches; as to be sober, courteous, diligent, patient, to honour all men. So, likewise, the Holy Spirit works the same in our hearts, not merely creating desires after holiness in general, but strongly inclining us to every particular grace, leading us to every individual part of 'whatever is admirable' (Phil. 4:8). And this with the greatest propriety: for as 'faith was made complete by what he did' (Jas. 2:22), so the completing or destroying the work of faith, and enjoying the favour, or suffering the displeasure, of God, greatly depends on every single act of obedience or disobedience.

Q 35 What is the fourth?

A Beware of sins of omission, lose no opportunity of doing good in any kind. Be zealous of good works, willingly omit no work, either of piety or mercy. Do all the good you possibly can to the bodies and souls of men. Particularly, 'you are never to reprove your neighbour or allow sin to fall on him.' Be active. Give no place to indolence or sloth, give no occasion to say, 'Lazy, that's what you are – lazy' (Exod. 5:17)! Many will say so still, but let your whole spirit and behaviour refute the slander. Be always employed, lose no shred of time, 'Gather the pieces that are left over' (John 6:12) so that nothing is lost. 'Whatever your hand finds to do, do it with all your might' (Eccles. 9:10). Be 'slow to speak' (Jas. 1:19), and wary in speaking. 'When words are many, sin is not absent' (Prov. 10:19). Do not talk much, neither long at a time. Few can converse profitably above an hour. Keep at the utmost distance from pious chit-chat, or religious gossiping.

Q 36 What is the fifth?

A Beware of desiring anything but God. Now you desire nothing else, every other desire is driven out, see that none enters again. 'Keep yourself pure', let your 'eye be good' and 'your whole body will be full of light' (see Luke 11:34). Admit no desire of pleasing food, or any other pleasure of sense; no desire of pleasing the eye or the imagination by anything grand, or new, or beautiful; no desire of money, of praise, or esteem; or happiness in any creature. You may bring these desires back, but you need not, you need feel them no more. It is for freedom that Christ has set you free. So stand firm (see Gal. 5:1).

Be patterns to all, of denying yourselves and taking up

your cross daily. Let them see that you make no account of any pleasure which does not bring you nearer to God, nor regard any pain which does, that you simply aim at pleasing him, whether by doing or suffering, that the constant language of your heart, with regard to pleasure or pain, honour or dishonour, riches or poverty, is,

> All's like to me, so I
> In my Lord may live and die!

Q 37 What is the sixth?

A Beware of schism, of making a division in the Church of Christ. That inward disunion, the members ceasing to have a reciprocal love an 'equal concern for each other' (1 Cor. 12:25), is the very root of all contention and every outward separation. Beware of everything tending thereto. Beware of a dividing spirit, shun whatever has the least appearance that way. Therefore, do not say, 'I follow Paul' or 'I follow Apollos' (1 Cor. 1:12), the very thing which caused the schism at Corinth. Do not say, 'This is my preacher, the best preacher in England. Give me him, and take all the rest.' All this tends to breed or foment division, to disunite those whom God has joined. Do not despise or run down any preacher, do not exalt any one above the rest, in case you hurt both him and God's cause. On the other hand, do not bear hard on any by reason for some incoherency or inaccuracy of expression, no, nor for some mistakes, were they really such.

Likewise, if you would avoid schism, observe every rule of the Society, and of the Bands, for the sake of conscience. Never omit meeting your Class or Band, never absent yourself from any public meeting. These are the very sinews of our Society, and whatever weakens, or tends to weaken, our regard for these, or our exactness in attending them, strikes at the very root of our community. As one says, 'That part of our economy, the private weekly meeting for prayer, examination, and particular exhortation, has been the greatest means of deepening and confirming every blessing that was received by the word preached, and of diffusing it to others, who could not attend the public ministry; whereas, without this religious connection and exchange between people, the most ardent attempts, by mere preaching, have proved of no lasting use.'

Suffer not one thought of separating from your brethren, whether their opinions agree with yours or not. Do not dream that any man sins in not believing you, in not taking your word; or that this or that opinion is essential to the work, and both must stand or fall together. Beware of impatience, of contradiction. Do not condemn or think in a hard way of those who cannot see just as you see, or who judge it their duty to contradict you, whether in a great thing or a small thing. I fear some of us have thought in a hard way of others, merely because they contradicted what we affirmed. All this tends to division, and, by everything of this kind, we are teaching them an evil lesson against ourselves.

O beware of touchiness, or testiness, not bearing to be spoken to, staring at the least word, and flying from those who do not implicitly receive mine or another's sayings!

Expect contradiction and opposition, together with crosses of various kinds. Consider the words of St Paul, 'it has been granted to you on behalf of Christ' for his sake, as a fruit of his death and intercession for you, 'not only to believe on him, but also to suffer for him' (Phil. 1:29). *It has been granted!* God gives you this opposition or reproach, it is a fresh token of his love. And will you disown the giver, or spurn his gift, and count it a misfortune? Will you not rather say, 'Father, the hour has come, that you may be glorified. Now you give your child to suffer something for you. Do with me according to your will'? Know that these things, far from being hindrances to the work of God, or to your soul, unless by your own fault, are not only unavoidable in the course of Providence, but profitable, yes, necessary, for you. Therefore, receive them from God (not from chance) with willingness, with thankfulness. Receive them from men with humility, meekness, submissiveness, gentleness, sweetness. Why should not even your outward appearance and manner be soft? Remember the character of Lady Cutts: 'It was said of the Roman Emperor Titus, never any one came displeased from him. But it might be said of her, Never any one went displeased to her: so secure were all of the kind and favourable reception which they would meet with from her.'

Beware of tempting others to separate from you. Give no offence which can possibly be avoided, see that your practice be in all things suitable to your profession, making the teaching about God our Saviour attractive. Be particularly careful in speaking of yourself. You may not, indeed, deny the work of God, but speak of it, when you are called thereto, in the most inoffensive manner possible. Avoid all magnificent, pompous words, indeed, you need give it no general name; neither perfection, sanctification, the second blessing, nor the having attained. Rather speak of the particulars which God has wrought for you. You may say, 'At such a time I felt a change which I am not able to express, and since that time, I have not felt pride, or self-will, or anger, or unbelief; nor anything but a fullness of love to God and to all mankind.' And answer any other plain question that is asked, with modesty and simplicity.

And if any of you should at any time fall from what you now are, if you should again feel pride or unbelief, or any temper from which you are now delivered; do not deny, do not hide, do not disguise it at all, at the peril of your soul. At all events go to one in whom you can confide, and speak just what you feel. God will enable him to speak a word in season, which shall be health to your soul. And surely he will again lift up your head, and cause the bones that have been broken to rejoice.

Q 38 What is the last advice that you would give them?

A Be exemplary in all things; particularly in outward things (as in dress), in little things, in spending your money (avoiding every needless expense), in deep, steady seriousness, and in the solidity and usefulness of all your conversation. So shall you be 'a light shining in a dark place' (2 Pet. 1:19). So will you daily 'grow in grace' until 'you will receive a rich welcome into the eternal kingdom of our Lord and Saviour Jesus Christ' (2 Pet. 1:11).

Most of the preceding advices are strongly enforced in the following reflections, which I recommend to your deep and frequent consideration, next to the holy scriptures:

1 The sea is an excellent figure of the fullness of God, and that of the blessed Spirit. For as the rivers all return into the sea; so the bodies, the souls, and the good works of the righteous return to God to live there in his eternal repose.

Although all the graces of God depend on his mere bounty, yet he is pleased generally to attach them to the prayers, the instructions and the holiness of those with whom we are. By strong though invisible attractions he draws some souls through their communication with others.

The sympathies formed by grace far surpass those formed by nature.

The truly devout show that passions as naturally flow from true as from false love, so deeply sensible are they of the goods and evils of those whom they love for God's sake. But this can only be comprehended by those who understand the language of love.

The bottom of the soul may be in repose, even while we are in many outward troubles, just as the bottom of the sea is calm while the surface is strongly agitated.

The best helps to growth in grace are found in unkind treatment, open insults, and the losses which happen to us. We should receive them with all thankfulness as preferable to all others, were it only on this account – that our will has no part in it.

The most rapid way to escape from our sufferings is to be willing they should endure as long as God pleases.

If we suffer persecution and affliction in a right manner, we attain a larger measure of conformity to Christ by a due improvement of one of these occasions, than we could have done merely by imitating his mercy, in abundance of good works.

One of the greatest evidences of God's love to those that love him is to send them afflictions with grace to bear them.

Even in the greatest afflictions, we ought to testify to God, that, in receiving them from his hand, we feel pleasure in the midst of the pain, from being afflicted by him who loves us and whom we love.

The most rapid way which God takes to draw a man to himself is to afflict him in that he loves most, and with good reason, and to cause this affliction to arise from some good action done with a single eye, because nothing can more clearly show him the emptiness of what is most lovely and desirable in the world.

2   True handing of oneself over to God's will consists in a thorough conformity to the whole will of God, who wills and does all (excepting sin) which comes to pass in the world. In order to do this we have only to embrace all events, good and bad, as he will.

In the greatest afflictions which can happen to the just, either from heaven or earth, they remain immovable in peace, and perfectly submissive to God, by an inward, loving regard to him, uniting in one all the powers of their souls.

We ought quietly to suffer whatever happens to us, to bear the defects of others and our own, to confess them to

God in secret prayer, or with groans that words cannot express; but never to speak a sharp or peevish word, nor to murmur or complain; but thoroughly willing that God should treat you in the manner that pleases him. We are his lambs, and therefore ought to be ready to suffer, even to death, without complaining.

We are to bear with those we cannot amend, and to be content with offering them to God. This is true handing ourselves over to God's will. And since God has borne our infirmities, we may well bear those of each other for his sake.

To abandon all, to strip one's self of all, in order to seek and to follow Jesus Christ naked to Bethlehem, where he was born; naked, to the hall where he was scourged, and naked to Calvary, where he died on the cross, is so great a mercy, that neither the thing, nor the knowledge of it, is given to any, but through faith in the Son of God.

3   There is no love of God without patience, and no patience without lowliness and sweetness of spirit.

Humility and patience are the surest proofs of the increase of love.

Humility alone unites patience with love, without which it is impossible to draw profit from suffering, or, indeed, to avoid complaint, especially when we think we have given no occasion for what men make us suffer.

True humility is a kind of self-annihilation, and this is the centre of all virtues.

A soul returned to God ought to be attentive to every-thing which is said to him on the subject of salvation with a desire to profit thereby.

Of the sins which God has pardoned, let nothing remain but a deeper humility in the heart, and a stricter regulation in our words, in our actions, and in our suffer-ings.

4   The person who bears and suffers evils with meek-ness and silence, is the sum of a Christian life.

God is the first object of our love: Its next office is to bear the defects of others. And we should begin the practice of this amid our own household.

We should chiefly exercise our love towards them who most shock either our way of thinking, or our frame of mind, or our knowledge, or the desire we have that others should be as virtuous as we wish to be ourselves.

5   God hardly gives his Spirit even to those whom he has established in grace, if they do not pray for it on all occasions, not only once but many times.

God does nothing but in answer to prayer: and even they who have been converted to God, without praying for it themselves (which is exceedingly rare), were not without the prayers of others. Every new victory which a soul gains is the effect of a new prayer.

On every occasion of uneasiness, we should retire to prayer, that we may give place to the grace and light of God, and then form our resolutions without being in any pain about what success they may have.

In the greatest temptations, a single look to Christ, and the bare pronouncing of his name, suffices to overcome the wicked one, so it be done with confidence and calmness of spirit.

God's command 'pray continually' (1 Thess. 5:17) is founded on the necessity we have of his grace to preserve the life of God in the soul, which can no more subsist one moment without it than the body can without air.

Whether we think of, or speak of, God, whether we act or suffer for him, all is prayer when we have no other objects than his love, and the desire of pleasing him.

All that a Christian does, even in eating and sleeping, is prayer, when it is done in simplicity, according to the order of God, without either adding to or diminishing from it by his own choice.

Prayer continues in the desire of the heart, though the understanding is employed on outward things.

In souls filled with love, the desire to please God is a continual prayer.

As the furious hate which the devil bears us is termed the roaring of a lion, so our vehement love may be termed crying after God.

God requires of his adult children only that their hearts be truly purified and that they offer him continually the wishes and vows that naturally spring from perfect love. For these desires, being the genuine fruits of love, are the most perfect prayers that can spring from it.

6   It is scarcely conceivable how straight the way is wherein God leads them that follow him, and how dependent we must be on him, unless we are lacking in our faithfulness to him.

It is hardly credible of how great consequences before God the smallest things are, and what great inconveniences sometimes follow those which appear to be small faults.

As a very little dust will disorder a clock, and the least sand will obscure our sight, so the least grain of sin which is on the heart will hinder its right motion towards God.

We ought to be in the church as the saints are in heaven, and in the house as the holiest men are in the church, doing our work in the house as we pray in the church, worshipping God from the ground of the heart.

We should be continually labouring to cut off all the useless things that surround us, and God usually retrenches the superfluities of our souls in the same proportion as we do those of our bodies.

The best means of resisting the devil is to destroy whatever of the world remains in us, in order to raise for God, on its ruins, a building all of love. Then shall we begin, in this fleeting life, to love God as we shall love him in eternity.

We scarce conceive how easy it is to rob God of his due, in our friendship with the most virtuous persons, until they are torn from us by death. But if this loss produce lasting sorrow, that is a clear proof that we had before two treasures, between which we divided our heart.

7 If, after having renounced all, we do not watch incessantly and beseech God to accompany our vigilance with his, we shall again be entangled and overcome.

As the most dangerous winds may enter at little openings, so the devil never enters more dangerously than by little unobserved incidents, which seem to be nothing, yet imperceptibly they open the heart to great temptations.

It is good to renew ourselves, from time to time, by closely examining the state of our souls, as if we had never done it before; for nothing tends more to the full assurance of faith than to keep ourselves by this means in humility, and the exercise of all good works.

To continual watchfulness and prayer ought to be added continual employment. For grace flees from a vacuum as well as nature; and the devil fills whatever God does not fill.

There is no faithfulness like that which ought to be between a guide of souls and the person directed by him. They ought continually to regard each other in God, and closely to examine themselves, whether all their thoughts are pure and all their words directed with Christian discretion. Other affairs are only the things of men, but these are particularly the things of God.

8 The words of St Paul, 'no-one can say, "Jesus is Lord," except by the Holy Spirit' (1 Cor. 12:3), show us the necessity of eyeing God in our good works, and even in our minutest thoughts, knowing that none is pleasing to him but those which he forms in us and with us. Hence we learn that we cannot serve him, unless he use our tongue, hands and heart, to do by himself and his Spirit whatever he would have us do.

If we are not utterly impotent, our good works would be our own property, whereas now they belong wholly to God, because they proceed from him and his grace: while raising our works and making them all divine, he

113

honours himself in us through them.

One of the principal rules in religion is, to lose no occasion of serving God. And, since he is invisible to our eyes, we are to serve him in our neighbour, which he receives as if done to himself in person, standing visibly before us.

God does not love men who are not steadfast, nor good works that are intermittent. Nothing is pleasing to him, but what resembles his own unchanging nature.

A constant attention to the work which God entrusts us with is a mark of consistent piety.

Love fasts when it can, and as much as it can. It leads to all the ordinances of God, and employs itself in all the outward works whereof it is capable. It flies, as it were, like Elijah over the plain, to find God on his holy mountain.

God is so great, that he communicates greatness to the least thing that is done for his service.

Happy are they who are sick, yes, or who lose their lives, for having done a good work.

God frequently conceals the part which his children have in the conversion of other souls. Yet one may boldly say, that a person who prays with groans too deep for words for a long time before God for the conversion of another, whenever that soul is converted to God, is one of the chief causes of it.

Love cannot be practised right unless we first exercise it the moment God gives the opportunity; and second, we cease the instant after to offer it to God by humble thanksgiving. And this for three reasons: First, to give to him what we have received from him. The second, to avoid the dangerous temptation which springs from the very goodness of these works. And the third, to unite ourselves to God, in whom the soul expands itself in prayer, with all the graces we have received and the good works we have done, to draw from him new strength against the bad effects which these very works may produce in us if we do not make use of the antidotes which God has ordained against these poisons. The true means to be filled anew with the riches of grace is thus to strip ourselves of it, and without this it is extremely difficult not to grow faint in the practice of good works.

Good works do not receive their last perfection till they, as it were, lose themselves in God. This is a kind of death to them, resembling that of our bodies, which will not attain their highest life, their immortality, till they lose themselves in the glory of our souls, or rather of God, wherewith they shall be filled. And it is only what they had of earthly and mortal, which good works lose by this spiritual death.

Fire is the symbol of love; and the love of God is the principle and the end of all our good works. But truth surpasses analogies; and the fire of divine love has this advantage over material fire, that it can return to its source, and raise thither with it all the good works which it produces. And by this means it prevents their being corrupted by pride, vanity, or any evil mixture. But this cannot be done otherwise than by making these good works in a spiritual manner die in God, by a deep gratitude which plunges the soul in him as in an abyss, with all that it is, and all the grace and works for which it is indebted to him, a gratitude whereby the soul seems to empty itself of them, that they may return to their source, as rivers seem willing to empty themselves when they pour themselves with all their waters into the sea.

When we have received any favour from God, we ought to retire, if not into our rooms, into our hearts and say, 'I come, Lord, to restore to you what you have given; and I freely relinquish it, to enter again into my own nothingness. For what is the most perfect creature in heaven or earth in your presence, but a void capable of being filled with you and by you, as the air which is void and dark is capable of being filled with the light of the sun, who withdraws it every day to restore it the next, there being nothing in the air that either appropriates this light or resists it? O give me the same facility of receiving and restoring your grace and good works! I say, *yours*, for I acknowledge the root from which they spring is in you, and not in me.'

26   Wesley's 1764 summary of Christian Perfection

In 1764, on a review of the whole subject, I wrote down the sum of what I had observed in the following short proposition:

1   There is such a thing as perfection, for it is again and again mentioned in scripture.

2   It is not so early as justification, for justified persons are to 'go on to maturity' ['go on unto perfection' AV] (Heb. 6:1).

3   It is not so late as death, for St Paul speaks of living men that were perfect (see Phil. 3:15).

4   It is not absolute. Absolute perfection belongs not to man, nor to angels, but to God alone.

5   It does not make a man infallible: None is infallible, while he remains in the body.

6   Is it sinless? It is not worth while to contend for a term. It is 'salvation from sin'.

7   It is 'perfect love' (see 1 John 4:18). This is the essence of it, its properties, or inseparable fruits, are always being joyful, praying continually, and giving thanks in all circumstances (see 1 Thess. 5:16–17).

8   It is improvable. It is so far from lying in an indivisible point, from being incapable of increase, that one perfected in love may grow in grace far swifter than he did before.

9   It is capable of being lost, of which we have numerous instances. But we were not thoroughly

convinced of this till five or six years ago.

10   It is constantly both preceded and followed by a gradual work.

11   But is it in itself instantaneous or not? In examining this, let us go on step by step.

An instantaneous change has been wrought in some believers. No one can deny this.

Since that change, they enjoy perfect love; they feel this, and this alone; they are 'always being joyful, praying continually, and giving thanks in all circumstances' (see 1 Thess. 5:16–18). Now, this is all that I mean by perfection; therefore, these are witnesses of the perfection which I preach.

But in some this change was not instantaneous. They did not perceive the instant when it was wrought. It is often difficult to perceive the instant when a man dies, yet there is an instant in which life ceases. And if even sin ceases, there must be a last moment of its existence, and a first moment of our deliverance from it.

'But if they have this love now, they will lose it.' They may, but they need not. And whether they do or not, they have it now; they now experience what we teach. They now are all love; they now rejoice, pray, and praise continually.

However, sin is only suspended in them, it is not destroyed. Call it which you please. They are all love today, and they 'do not worry about tomorrow' (Matt. 6:34).

But this doctrine has been much abused. So has that of justification by faith. But this is no reason for giving up either this or any other scriptural doctrine. You must not throw away the baby with the bathwater!

But those who think they are saved from sin say they have no need of the beneficial work of Christ. They say just the contrary. Their language is:

Every moment, Lord, I want
The merit of thy death!

They never before had so deep, so inexpressible a conviction of the need of Christ in all his beneficial works as they have now.

Therefore, all our preachers should make a point of preaching perfection to believers constantly, strongly and explicitly; and all believers should mind this one thing, and continually agonise for it.

27 Perfection is a doctrine of the New Testament

I have now done what I proposed. I have given a plain and simple account of the manner in which I first received the doctrine of perfection, and the sense in which I received, and do receive, and teach it to this day. I have declared the whole and every part of what I mean by that scriptural expression. I have drawn the picture of it at full length, without either disguise or covering. And I would now ask any impartial person: What is there so frightful in it? From where is all this outcry, which, for these twenty years and more, has been made throughout the kingdom; as if all Christianity were destroyed and all religion torn up by the roots? Why is it, that the very name of perfection has been cast out of the mouths of Christians, yes, exploded and abhorred, as if it contained the most pernicious heresy? Why have the preachers of it been laughed at, like mad dogs, even by men that fear God; and even by some of their own children, some whom they, under God, had given new birth through the gospel? What reason is there for this, or what pretence? Reason, sound reason, there is none. It is impossible there should be any reason. But pretences there are, and those in great abundance. Indeed, there is ground to fear that with some who treat us thus it is mere pretence, that it is no more than a copy of their ill-will, from the beginning to the end. They wanted, they sought, occasion against me, and here they found what they sought.

This is Mr Wesley's doctrine! He preaches perfection! He does, yet this is not his doctrine any more than it is yours, or any one else's, who is a minister of Christ. For it is his doctrine, particularly, emphatically his. It is the doctrine of Jesus Christ. Those are his words, not mine: 'Be perfect, therefore, as your heavenly Father is perfect' (Matt. 5:48). And who says you shall not, or, at least, not until your soul is separated from the body? It is the doctrine of St Paul, the doctrine of St James, of St Peter and St John; and also it is Mr Wesley's doctrine, just as it is the doctrine of every one who preaches the pure and whole gospel. I tell you, as plain as I can speak, where and when I found this. I found it in the words of God, in the Old and New Testament, when I read them with no other view or desire but to save my own soul. But whosesoever this doctrine is, I pray you, what harm is there in it? Look at it again, survey it on every side, and that with the closest attention. In one view, it is purity of intention, dedicating all the life to God. It is the giving to God of all our heart, it is one desire and design ruling all our tempers. It is the devoting, not a part but all our soul, body and substance to God. In another view, it is all the mind which was in Christ, enabling us to walk as Christ walked. It is the circumcision of the heart from all obscenity, all inward as well as outward pollution. It is a renewal of the heart in the whole image of God, the full likeness of him who created it. In yet another, it is the loving God with all our heart, and our neighbour as ourselves.

Now, take it in which of these views you please (for there is no material difference), and this is the whole and sole perfection, as a train of writings prove to a demonstration, which I have believed and taught for these forty years, from 1725 to 1765.

28 Wesley commends the doctrine of perfection

Let this perfection appear in its original form, and who can speak one word against it? Will any dare to speak against loving the Lord our God with all our heart, and our neighbour as ourselves; against a renewal of heart, not only in part but in the whole image of God? Who will speak against being purified from all pollution, bodily and spiritual; or against having all the mind that was in Christ, and walking in every way as Christ walked? Which person who calls himself a Christian, has the audacity to object to our devoting, not a part, but all of our soul, body, and possessions to God? Which thinking person would object to all our heart's being given to God, and having a single aim governing our complete frame of mind? I say again, allow this perfection to be seen for what it is, and who will oppose it?

It must be falsified before it can be opposed. It must be dressed up in a bear-skin first, before the wildest people will scarcely be induced to worry about it. But whatever these people do, do not let the children of God fight any longer against the image of God. Let not the members of Christ say anything against having the whole mind that was in Christ. Do not let those who are alive to God oppose those who dedicate all their lives to God. Why should you who have his love poured out in your heart (see Rom. 5:5) withhold giving him all your heart? Does not all that is within you cry out, 'Of those who love, who can love enough?' What pity it is that those who desire and aim to please God should have any other aim or desire! So why should they fear having this one desire and aim ruling their complete frame of mind, as if it were a fatal delusion; why do they hate it, as if it were an abomination to God? Why should devout men be afraid of devoting their complete souls, bodies, and possessions to God? Why should those who love Christ reckon it a mistake worthy of being condemned for, to think we may have the complete mind that was in him?

We agree with and campaign for the doctrine that we are justified freely because of the righteousness and blood of Christ. So why do you oppose us so fiercely? Is it because you expect to be sanctified in the same way, wholly through the Spirit? We do not look for any favours either from the open sinners, or from those who have only the appearance of religion. So how long will you who worship God in spirit, who are 'circumcised . . . not with a circumcision done by the hands of men' (Col. 2:11), draw swords with those who seek an entire circumcision of heart, who thirst to be purifed 'from everything that contaminates body and spirit' and to perfect 'holiness out of reverence for God' (2 Cor. 7:1)? Are we your enemies, because we look for a full deliverance from that 'sinful mind which is hostile to God' (Rom. 8:7)? No, we are your brethren, your fellow-labourers in the vineyard of the Lord, your companions in the kingdom and suffering of Jesus. Although we believe this, (if we are fools in this, then bear with us as fools), we do expect to love God with all our heart, and our neighbour as ourselves. Yes, we do believe, that he will in this world so 'cleanse the thoughts of our hearts, by the inspiration of his Holy Spirit, that we shall perfectly love him, and worthily magnify his holy name' (Book of Common Prayer. The Lord's Supper or Holy Communion, The Collect).

Brief Thoughts on Christian Perfection

Some thoughts occurred to my mind this morning about Christian Perfection, and the nature and time of receiving it, which I believe may be useful to set down.

1   By perfection I mean the humble, gentle, patient love of God and our neighbour, ruling our minds, words and actions.

I do not include an impossibility of falling from it, either in part or in whole. Therefore, I retract several expressions in our hymns, which partly express, party imply, such an impossibility.

And I do not contend for the term *sinless*, though I do not object against it.

2   As to the manner, I believe this perfection is always wrought in the soul by a simple act of faith, consequently, in an instant.

But I believe a gradual work, both preceding and following that instant.

3   As to the time, I believe this instant generally is the instant of death, the moment before the soul leaves the body. But I believe it may be ten, twenty, or forty years before.

I believe it is usually many years after justification, but that it may be within five years or five months after it. I know no conclusive argument to the contrary.

If it must be many years after justification, I should be glad to know how many. *Pretium quotus arroget annus?* (How many years give sanction to our lines? [Horace])

And how many days or months, or even years, can any one allow to be between perfection and death? How far from justification must it be, and how near to death?

London, January 27th, 1767

The Hodder and Stoughton Christian Classics Series

The Hodder and Stoughton Christian Classics are original translations, adaptations or abridgements of the great classics of devotional spirituality. Chosen for their reference to the needs of today's Christians, for their theological and spiritual perception and for the timelessness of their message, each of the titles in the series will enrich the faith of the reader.

The Confessions of St Augustine
New Translation with an Introduction by
E. M. Blaiklock

The Cloud of Unknowing
Edited by Halcyon Backhouse

The Twelve Steps of Humility and Pride
On Loving God
Bernard of Clairvaux

The Little Flowers of St Francis
Translated by E. M. Blaiklock and A. C. Keyes

The Institutes of Christian Religion
John Calvin

The Practice of the Presence of God
Brother Lawrence

The Greatest Thing in the World
Henry Drummond